CHRISTIAN FAITH AND
POLITICAL HOPES

Christian Faith and Political Hopes

A REPLY TO E. R. NORMAN

Charles Elliott
Duncan B. Forrester
Peter Hinchliff
Daniel Jenkins
David Jenkins
John Kent
James Mark
Robert Moore
Haddon Willmer

LONDON
EPWORTH PRESS

Enquiries should be addressed to
The Methodist Publishing House
Wellington Road
Wimbledon
London SW19 8EU

7162 0329 4

Printed in Great Britain by
The Garden City Press Limited
Letchworth, Hertfordshire SG6 1JS

Contents

Acknowledgements

Extracts from Dr Norman's Reith Lectures are used by permission of the author and of the Oxford University Press, publishers of *Christianity and the World Order* by Edward Norman.

Extracts from *Church and Society in England 1770—1970* are used by permission of the author and the publisher, Clarendon Press.

The extract from 'Little Gidding' is taken from *Collected Poems 1909—1962* by T. S. Eliot and is used by permission of Faber and Faber Ltd.

Introduction

To Say Something Positive

THIS book is a response to the Reith Lectures given by the Reverend Dr E. R. Norman and printed in *The Listener* between 2 November and 7 December 1978. The essays in it were all written before the lectures were published as a book by Oxford University Press in March 1979.

The writers were disappointed by much that Dr Norman said, more perhaps by what he did not say and most of all by the perspective and spirit he gave to the discussion of 'Christianity and World Order'. There is no need to elaborate on the disquiets which first provoked us to think of making a public response in this way, for the essays make them plain enough.

From the beginning we have been agreed that we did not wish to get lost in criticizing and refuting Dr Norman's lectures in detail. We should then run the risk of not doing justice to much that is of value in them. It is important to recognize and to deal with some genuine issues Dr Norman raises; it is not enough to show how badly phrased the questions are and leave it at that. So our purpose was to make a positive response. There can, in a controversy like this, be no positive without a negative, but we have tried to see that the positive predominates. We hope we have made it possible for our readers to be more interested in engaging with the life of the world in ways that may deservedly be called Christian than in the little local difficulty of our disagreement with the Dean of Peterhouse.

What, then, is our positive word? This book has not come out of long discussion amongst us. Each writer is responsible only for his own essay and at the level of detail the book has no unified message. All the same, positive patterns do emerge from the interweaving of leading ideas, concerns and experiences.

We live amid the harsh realities of politics. The Church cannot allow its alleged political incompetence to be an excuse for inactivity. As Hinchliff argues, it is good for it, in witnessing for human values, to be uncompromising to the point of naïvety. Often, as examples analysed by Forrester and Moore show, the attempt to preach or live an apolitical Gospel has led the Church into more political ways, just to be true to itself. If Christians in India discovered that road, for example, why do we hesitate in Britain? Are we to stand for human rights in the world and not notice how they are violated in our own country? Daniel Jenkins presses the point home by asking how a Christian assessment of the state of Britain should be made and what kind of help the churches should give to politicians.

Evidently, we are searching for positive ways of relating faith and politics even though they do not easily fit together. Mark reminds us that we must understand what is happening in the modern world and that religion is significant for politics precisely because it is concerned with what transcends it. A notable characteristic of the modern world is our ability deliberately to create wealth and to envisage the abolition of suffering. By way of an assessment of Dr Norman's interpretation of the history of Anglican social thinking, Kent suggests that, after Marx, the choice between enduring and abolishing suffering has become a theological crux, disturbing for any complacent orthodoxy. And, according to Elliot, we cannot explain politically-caused suffering by reference to impersonal evil alone but must make it a matter of human responsibility by talking of structural sin. Thus the political is to be brought within the terms and scope of faith as it is focused in the life, death and resurrection of Jesus of Nazareth. Willmer contends that redemption not the fall provides the perspective in which Christians should view politics. In sum, as David Jenkins concludes, Christian faith impels us into politics with good reasons; properly understood it leaves us no choice in many situations. But to say that is not to change the essence of Christianity into politics: it is to be finding through political involvement more of the reality of the God whom the Gospel leads us to trust and hope for.

HADDON WILLMER

The Contributors

Charles Elliott is Professor of Development Policy and Planning at the University College of Swansea. An Anglican priest, he has lived in Zambia and conducted research in a large number of developing countries. He was for a time on the staff of the Committee established by the WCC and the Vatican to spearhead their common interest in issues of world development and peace. For the last three years, he has been Special Adviser to the House of Commons Select Committee on Overseas Development. He has written on Christian ethics with particular reference to the issues of world poverty and inequality.

Duncan B. Forrester is Professor of Christian Ethics and Practical Theology at the University of Edinburgh. He was for eight years an educational missionary, teaching politics at Madras Christian College in South India, and then lectured in politics in the School of African and Asian Studies at the University of Sussex as well as being Chaplain of the University. His publications are concerned with Indian politics and theology, the history of political theology and the sociology of missions. His book *Caste and Christianity* is to be published in 1979.

Peter Hinchliff was born in South Africa in 1929. He was professor of church history at a university in that country from 1960 to 1969 and was a member of the governing body of the Federal Theological Seminary of Southern Africa. He was also, between 1964 and 1974, a member of the Faith and Order Commission of the World Council of Churches. He came to Britain in 1969 to be secretary to the

Board for Mission and Unity of the General Synod of the Church of England, the department responsible for ecumenical affairs including liaison with the World Council of Churches. He is the author of the standard history of the Anglican Church in South Africa and of *The One-Sided Reciprocity,* a study of the relationship between Church and State in England. He has been a fellow of Balliol College, Oxford, since 1972.

Daniel Jenkins is minister of Regent Square United Reformed Church, London WC1, and formerly taught at the Universities of Chicago and Sussex. He has written many books about the Christian faith in relation to modern society, including *Equality and Excellence* (1961) and *The British: Their Identity and their Religion* (1975).

David Jenkins was Fellow and Chaplain of the Queen's College, Oxford from 1954–69 (Bampton Lecturer, Oxford University, 1966); 1969–73 Director, Humanum Studies, World Council of Churches, Geneva; 1973–8 (from 1979 Joint-) Director, William Temple Foundation, Manchester (Research in Christian Social Ethics). Since January 1979, Professor of Theology and Head of the Department of Theology and Religious Studies, University of Leeds.

John Kent is professor of Theology at Bristol University. A Methodist, he has written widely on nineteenth-century religious history, and published *Holding the Fort, Studies in Victorian Revivalism* (Epworth Press, London) in 1978.

James Mark is Joint Editor of the journal *Theology.* He was Assistant Secretary, HM Treasury, and Under Secretary at the Ministry of Overseas Development until 1974. He has been active as a lay theologian for many years and has written on economic and financial questions, especially

overseas development and on Bonhoeffer, Simone Weil,
Sartre, Bultmann and themes in philosophical theology.

Robert Moore was born in 1936 and served in the Royal
Navy for several years until 1960. He is a graduate of the
Universities of Hull and Durham. He did research on race
relations in Birmingham in 1964–5 and since then has been
writing mainly on immigration policy. He is interested in
the sociology of religion and is active in the field of human
rights and anti-apartheid concerns. He served on the BCC
committee on Migration. Since 1976 he has been Professor
of Sociology at the University of Aberdeen.

Haddon Willmer read History and Theology at Cambridge
and since 1966 has taught Theology and Church history at
the University of Leeds. From 1975 to 1977 he was the first
Maurice Reckitt Research Fellow in Christian Social
Thought at the University of Sussex, making a theological
appraisal of parliamentary politics and developing a theory
of the 'politics of forgiveness'. A Baptist layman, he is
concerned for the political service of local Christian
churches.

Peter Hinchliff

Religion and Politics: The Harsh Reality

We have seen the Anglican Primate [of Cape Town] in his
sacerdotal robes, with his mitre on his head and his crozier in his
hand, leap into the bloody arena of war-politics, and there lay
about him like a gladiator. No words of peace from him. Kill!
Kill! Kill! is his cry.[1]

THIS is *not* a quotation from Edward Norman's Reith
lectures: it appeared in a Cape colonial newspaper during
the Boer war. It was, in fact, a very unfair, as well as an
unintentionally funny, attack on the prelate in question for
'interfering in politics'. And it reflected the unease and
distaste with which the average man in the street reacts to
ecclesiastics who make political pronouncements. Religion, the average man believes, is a private affair relating not
to *this* world but to another (if there is one). Politics is a
dirty game in which the Church ought not to become
involved, since the Church ought to be keeping its hands
clean. Clergymen should be men of peace not of controversy, faction and violence: they are also somewhat
impractical men who should leave practical affairs to those
who understand them. It is, in any case, unfair to use the
privileged authority of the pulpit to propound a party line.

These are largely emotional reactions, not rational or
logically consistent opinions, but they are none the less real
and Norman's lectures appeared to provide them with
a respectable rationale. His criticisms of the 'politicization'

[1] M. H. M. Wood, *Father in God,* Macmillan 1913, pp. 355 f.

of Christianity, of the World Council of Churches' grants to liberation movements, of the lack of political expertise exhibited by ecclesiastical leaders, of the divisiveness of religion in politics, and of the socialist bias of much theological and religious writing, seemed to be a scholarly and coherent justification for the instinctive feeling of the layman.

In fact, however, Norman has been misunderstood. By 'politicization' he means substituting political *goals and purposes* for religious ones, evacuating religion of its eternal concerns. He was not, at least at first, attacking those Christians who take politics seriously, but only those who talk and act as if the Church's business was *primarily* a political one rather than the saving of souls. Hence his stress upon original sin and the corruption of human nature. If man is naturally evil, human society is necessarily imperfect. No amount of striving will create a just society. The Church ought to concentrate on the religious redemption of human beings and on bringing them to the eternal and perfect society in heaven.

Much of this is clearly right. A politicized Christianity (in Norman's sense) is doomed to failure. Real Christianity is concerned with a person, Jesus Christ. He is the true human being—the goal, the pattern, the path to perfection, the source of the power to become good, the motivating force, the mould for all humanity. When commitment to a political or social programme is substituted for commitment to this person, one of two dangerous consequences tends to follow. Either one finds oneself crushed by a terrible sense of guilt because one cannot reform the society to which one belongs and so is somehow responsible for its injustices and cruelties, or one projects that guilt as a hatred of those whom one can identify as the enemies of justice, freedom and human dignity. What one is really doing, in fact, is to forget that forgiveness is the only real answer to sin. One's own share in the sin of society can only cease to be a crushing burden when one is prepared to accept forgiveness. Other people's share in that sin needs to be forgiven, too: one has to hate the sin not the sinner.

There is a further problem for a Christianity in which the creation of a perfect secular society in this world is the real purpose for which the Church exists. It is self-contradictory. The goal is unlikely to be reached very soon (granting that it can be reached at all). The generations of human beings who struggle and suffer, and are sacrificed, along the road to that goal do not participate in the final 'salvation' of mankind. They are merely the means towards the desired end. But a politicized Christianity takes as its premise the belief that all men are entitled to be treated as human beings with needs that *must* be met. If countless generations simply become stepping stones for the benefit of the possibly fortunate survivors, *their* needs are never met. They are not treated as fully human. Whatever goal the Church has, whatever 'salvation' may mean, it has to be something which is, in principle, available to each member of each generation. A secular 'salvation', the creation of a perfect political society, has nothing to offer in the meanwhile.

But, of course, a 'politicized' Christianity is very different from a Christianity which takes political affairs seriously, and this is where Norman has been misunderstood. It may be that he has only himself to blame, for in his later lectures he began to speak as if he thought that the Church should have nothing to do with politics at all. But his original thesis was that it is not the business of ecclesiastical leaders to make political pronouncements, propose political solutions or take political action. That is to be left to those who understand the practical realities of politics. And this is quite different from the pietist position Norman has been accused of adopting. Pietists *have* maintained that the only thing that matters is the eternal world and that one ought to opt out of the affairs of this world altogether. The very different view that no human society can be perfect and that government ought to be left in the hands of those who possess the necessary expertise, and whose wisdom is to be trusted, is the traditional position of right-wing or politically conservative Christians.[2] If those in power are themselves Christians, one may hope that their actions will be governed by more or less moral considerations. And this is indeed a way of saying that the Church *should* be involved in politics, not through the pronouncements of prelates or synods, but through the activities of Christian politicians.

To anyone belonging to this tradition, the World Council of Churches' 'Programme to Combat Racism' will, understandably, seem to be a particularly unpleasant example of the wrong kind of dabbling in dangerous politics. It is also exactly the kind of thing that the average British layman finds literally shocking because it seems to be encouraging and financing bloodshed and violence. But it is naïvely academic to argue that it is an example of the way in which a 'liberal', unorthodox or modernist theology leads to a politicized Christianity, to an alliance with extreme left-wing socialism and so to the manipulation of trendy but inexperienced ecclesiastics by the forces of revolution. Even if the facts supported the argument in the case of the wcc, which they do not, it is equally naïve and academic to think that some neat intellectual theory will apply to and explain a wide variety of different cases. Attempts by Russian Orthodox Christians to come to terms with a Communist state, of which Norman made a great deal in his third lecture, obviously follow a completely different pattern. Orthodox theology is very conservative, traditional and other-worldly, not at all politicized or secular. The view· that prevails in Russia is, in fact, much more like the attitude that Norman seems to advocate—politics is for the

[2] This is brought out very clearly by Anthony Quinton, *The Politics of Imperfection,* Faber 1978.

politicians, the Church's job is to save souls: the Church ought to operate within the *status quo* and not seek to overturn it. That the political *status quo* in Russia happens to be left wing rather than right wing does not alter the fact that it is the 'conservative' rather than the 'radical' model of the relationship between religion and politics which really applies. The Russian Church even tends to produce those shrewdly political 'prince-bishops' whose acumen Norman seemed at one stage to admire. It is a little unfair to criticize them because they happen to live in a twentieth-century Soviet state rather than in medieval England.

Even in the case of the wcc Programme to Combat Racism the neat theoretical model about modernist theology, politicized Christianity, trendy bishops and socialist tendencies, does not really stand up. The decision to set up the Programme was indeed the outcome of a challenge delivered at the Fourth Assembly of the World Council at Uppsala in 1968, when some delegates expressed impatience with mere resolutions against racial discrimination and asked for direct action instead. The idea received form at the meeting of the Central Committee at Canterbury in 1969, when the Programme was actually set up, but it was not until the specific grants were allocated in the following year that it attracted much publicity.

On the surface, admittedly, there appears to be a simple progression from theory to practice but the World Council is not an ecclesiastical parliament. The Assembly, consisting of some 600 members, meets only once in about five years. It has no regular, continuing existence. Each assembly is really a separate entity, though a good many familiar faces appear again and again. It does not possess any authority over the member churches and it cannot commit them, in spite of the fact that the delegates are all appointed by those churches. It is also, in the last resort, financially dependent on the churches so that it cannot take any action without the backing at least of the wealthiest members (and that means the Western European and North American churches).

In any organization the decision-making processes are determined by a complex of factors which derive from its history, from its structure and constitution, from the interplay of personalities and from psychological factors, as well as from political, theological or other theories. And the complex of factors will, of course, be peculiar to that particular organization. How a decision on policy, taken at a theoretical and rather abstract level, becomes actual practice will depend very largely on these factors.

The Central Committee (some 100 strong) and its executive meet more frequently than the Assembly and are responsible for seeing that the often very general resolutions of an Assembly come to some sort of practical reality. But even these bodies, carefully chosen to provide for as wide a denominational, geographical and racial spectrum as possible, are too large to be effective policy-making agencies. There is nothing which corresponds to a cabinet; the permanent staff of the wcc has to fulfil a very difficult role as both a kind of civil service, administering the machine, and as an agency which enables policy to become articulate. It is the staff which has to identify the intention of the resolutions and turn them (with the assistance of the standing commissions of the World Council, subcommittees of the Central Committee, *ad hoc* consultative bodies and individual advisers) into actual *structures* which will win not only the formal approval of the Central Committee but also the moral and financial support of the widely varied member churches.

Every administrative staff, whether it is a national civil service or the ecclesiastical equivalent, tends to recruit at a level of ability which is really slightly higher than the job actually requires. It does so partly because a high level of ability is undoubtedly required in order to translate policy into actual practical mechanics, and partly because the job is likely to have the status to attract able candidates. But since the *making* of policy is never (at least in theory) in the hands of the permanent officials, their ability is never fully used at a creative level. In an industrial organization a similar ability usually has the opportunity of rising through middle management to senior management and of becoming, in the end, part of the policy-making, decision-taking body. In a civil service it does not: policy is made by the politicians. So there is always an element of unused creativity or originality. Hence the stories that continually go the rounds about permanent officials who hope that no minister will stay much more than two years[3] because that gives civil servants an influence on policy which they do not have when the politician really knows his portfolio. In the wcc there is no 'minister'. Administrative officials *have* to formulate policy and they cannot take refuge in the anonymity required of civil servants for they have to take a measure of public responsibility for what is done. At the same time the degree of self-effacement required from these very able people, if they are not to exceed their official role, is enormous. In practice it is their thinking which is likely to be reflected in policies and structures more than that of anyone else. It is not so much that the staff can, or would seek to, compel the representative bodies to adopt policies against their will, as that there is no alternative agency by which the policies can be formulated. If the staff does not happen to design a particular way of doing things, there really is little possibility of that way being considered. This is inevitable, for if a large deliberative or legislative body rejects a detailed piece of planning (like a budget, for instance), it is simply incapable of substituting something of its own.

The way in which a permanent administrative staff behaves is almost invariably governed by a set of conven-

[3] See e.g. Anthony Howard, quoting Richard Crossman, in *The Times,* 13 November 1978.

tions which are, in turn, the product of its history. Historically the wcc is the result of an amalgamation of two quite different organizations (the Faith and Order Movement and the Universal Christian Council for Life and Work) which were later joined by a third (the International Missionary Council). Faith and Order was born before the First World War and was to be a forum for the discussion of the theological issues which divided the churches. In order to exist at all it had to proclaim its strict neutrality from the start. All theological traditions had to be treated as equally valid. No standard of orthodoxy could be laid down in advance. Each church which wished to join had to be accepted on its own terms: the only doctrinal prerequisite was belief in '. . . our Lord Jesus Christ as God and Saviour'. And the movement had to renounce any intention of compelling or authority to compel any church to alter its beliefs or practices, or to impose a union upon its member churches.

Life and Work came into existence between the wars. Its object was to demonstrate that Christianity was supranational and possessed a unity of values and morality which was more important that the divisions of nationalism or economic class. It was to serve as an expression of an international Christian conscience and to concern itself with the social aspects of the gospel. It was, therefore, from the very start, committed to the belief that Christianity had a part to play in political issues. Moreover, since it dealt with matters of social morality (on which Christians were thought to be more or less agreed) it could expect to speak with a single voice on peace, international justice, poverty, unemployment, totalitarianism and freedom—all the issues that were prominent in the thirties. It could hope to unite Christians on these issues in a way which Faith and Order had specifically been compelled to renounce in the area of theology.

In 1937 each of the two movements passed resolutions which, in effect, merged them in a 'world council of churches in process of formation'. By the time the Second World War broke out there was an embryo organization and the beginnings of a staff, with Visser t'Hooft as the general secretary of the provisional committee. The fragile amalgam of the different traditions of the two movements was very early subjected to a severe test. Dietrich Bonhoeffer appealed to embryo organization to condemn those German Christians who temporized with the Nazi regime and to recognize the 'confessing Church' as the only true representative of Christianity in Germany. Though perhaps no one realized it, Bonhoeffer was really appealing to the Life and Work tradition against that of Faith and Order, to a united Christian conscience against the neutral acceptance of each church on its own terms. It was too soon to ask for such a decision and no action was taken. In effect, the Faith and Order tradition was followed.

Many of the leaders of the ecumenical movement, however, and particularly those who were, or were to become, office-bearers or members of staff of the wcc, were deeply involved in the struggle against Nazism during the war. It was especially the influence of Karl Barth, and the importance of his disciples within the staff of the embryo organization, which set a particular stamp upon the style of thought associated with ecumenical political activity.[4] It is for this reason that it is sheer nonsense to argue that the wcc represents a politicized Christianity resulting from a secular theology. Barth's theology was the very reverse of secular: it was orthodox, neo-Calvinist, stressing the fallen-ness of man, the sovereignty of the transcendent God, the other-worldliness of salvation, and the autonomy of theology. But Barth was also (though this is less often remembered) a Christian socialist and his rejection of liberal protestantism was, in fact, a reaction against its theology

[4] Peter W. Ludlow, 'The International Protestant Community in the Second World War', *Journal of Ecclesiastical History,* July 1978, Vol. 29, pp. 311 ff. and n.b. p. 336.

of human progress. The cruelties and the injustices of the political structures of twentieth-century Germany were proof of man's continuing corruption. But they were also a challenge to the Christian conscience.

The development of the WCC campaign against racism was much more a continuation of this tradition and style of theology, than of politicization in the strict sense in which Norman first used it. It was Visser t'Hooft, one of the 'Barthians' and principal member of the WCC staff for more than a quarter of a century, who described racism as a 'moral heresy' in the debates leading up to the creation of the Programme in 1969. 'Moral heresy' is admittedly a concept of somewhat dubious theological worth, but it is easy to understand why men who had supported resistance movements in Europe throughout the war years were particularly susceptible to the argument that it was hypocritical of white Western Christians to adopt a pacifist and non-violent stance when they were asked to give similar assistance to black liberation movements in white-dominated southern Africa.

This is not to say that there were no other theological factors in the decision to set up the Programme. The sixties were admittedly the period when a secular 'death-of-God' theology was attracting attention and it is even possible that some of the staid, respectable and mostly middle-aged-to-elderly ecclesiastics composing the Central Committee were influenced by it. It was also a period when it was beginning to be realized that the Faith and Order approach to unity was going to be a much slower process than had once been hoped. A single, united Church, created by theological agreement was going to be a long time coming, yet federalism had been rejected as a second-best which would prevent the ideal from ever being realized. United Christian action on the basis of 'middle axioms'[5]

[5] '. . . half way between general principles, which are easily accepted because they have no empirical content, and detailed policies, which depend on so many empirical factors that a consensus is unlikely—Ronald Preston in *Theology*, November 1978, Vol. LXXXI, p. 441.

(i.e. essentially the Life and Work approach) seemed particularly attractive.

Even more important, perhaps, was the fact that this was also the period when delegates from the Third World began to play a much more active and prominent part in WCC affairs. Their resentment of the after-effects of former colonialism (political and economic) was very strong and it was in no sense something borrowed from a politicized theology of the West. Representatives of the Eastern-bloc Orthodox churches had also just begun to regard themselves as a real part of the ecumenical movement, having overcome their suspicion of the way American money dominated the finances of the WCC, and the inherited sense of resentment at what some Orthodox had suffered at the hands of the 'imperialism' of Western Protestant missionaries. They were only too glad to find an issue on which they could whole-heartedly, and with a clear conscience, take a line which would be favourably regarded by their own governments.

In spite of the many justifiable criticisms which can be levelled at this and other attempts to express a Christian mind on social and political issues it is clear, when one examines the case in some detail, that it is absurd to generalize in a facile way about 'politicization' and its causes. The factors that have to be taken into account are many and varied, and are often peculiar to the particular example. Even in the allegedly paradigm case, it is not clear whether 'politicization' is, strictly speaking, an applicable term or, if it is, whether it is in any real sense a result of an abandonment of traditional and other-worldly dogmatic positions. It is not even clear that it is the result of the trendiness of politically naïve ecclesiastics, for it must be remembered that in at least one dramatic instance the WCC proved to be better informed in political affairs than the supposed political experts. When grants were made to Frelimo, not for military purposes but on the grounds that it effectively controlled a large part of Portuguese East Africa and was, therefore, responsible for schools, hospitals and the general welfare of the population, the political experts rejected this claim as nonsense. The Portuguese, they said, were far too firmly entrenched for the wcc report to be true. The sudden and total collapse of the colonial administration showed, without doubt, who had been the better informed.

An entirely different set of factors operates in South Africa or Latin America and it is insensitive to suggest that political pronouncements and political activities in those contexts are likely to be the result of a desire on the part of churchmen to embrace a trendy socialism. Over and over again, Christians who have been almost entirely apolitical find themselves *driven* into protest and action because human beings are hurt by unjust laws and harsh, tyrannical governments. A former dean of Johannesburg, whose theology was a very conservative, very orthodox, Anglo-Catholicism, and who had never been a political activist, undertook to look after the dependants of political prisoners and was eventually to be convicted of all sorts of 'treasonable' offences. In circumstances like these it is not enough to tell one's conscience that political things are best left to those who understand them, or that, after all, injustice and cruelty do not prevent a man's soul from being saved. No Christian moralist has ever been willing to say that obedience to the state is an over-riding obligation. Even Hensley Henson, whom Norman (in another context)[6] seems to regard as almost the only non-trendy English bishop between the wars, and whose Gifford lectures were, in effect, directed against 'Christian socialism', made the point very clearly. '. . . Christian morality can never be merely conventional, endorsing the obligations which social custom or public law may prescribe'—and '. . . the

[6] Edward Norman, *Church and Society in England, 1770–1970*, Clarendon Press 1976, pp. 326 ff.

Christian can never yield an unqualified submission to any secular authority'.[7] Protest against injustice need not, therefore, necessarily be either a politically left wing nor a theologically secularizing action. But it can be a very lonely and very frightening thing and if it produces theological heart-searchings or alliances with surprising political groups that is, perhaps, understandable.

The Christian Church is, by its nature, concerned with people. Nor is it simply its theological nature which so commits it. Its practical nature, as a network of local communities in which a pastoral care and a mutual love are continually being expressed, involve it in the lives of human beings. Politicians, public servants and academics can concern themselves with 'the population' or 'society' or other abstractions of that kind. The Christian pastor can not. He has to deal with, and care for, people. If he cares for those who are casualties of an unjust system, he will feel compelled to try and prevent the continuation of the system. Other people may say, 'Of course we do not like the fact that so many prisoners seem to fall out of fourth-storey windows, but after all the security police know what they are doing'. It is doubtful whether a Christian can take such a line. If, frightened, lonely, agonized and (no doubt) politically naïve, he tries to do something about it, it is intolerably smug to condemn him as a divisive influence upon society or as the exponent of a false, trendy, quasi-Marxist and politicized Christianity. If a theological conservative like Barth and a political conservative like Henson could recognize that a Christian both *has* political responsibilities yet cannot give unqualified obedience to the state, it is absurd to argue that political action is usually the result of secularizing the gospel or embracing a trendy socialism.

In any case the Church is not composed solely of bishops and clergymen and its voice is not heard through the

[7] Herbert Hensley Henson, *Christian Morality,* Clarendon Press 1936, p. 246.

pronouncements of synods alone. The Church is the whole people of God and the layman has at least something of the same duty to care for other people as the clergyman. Since Christians are also citizens, the Church cannot 'go into politics': it is there already, by virtue of the fact that Christians have votes to exercise, if for no other reason. In this, of course, it differs from the Church of the New Testament and, if the New Testament has very little say about the positive political obligations of Christians (other than obedience), it is because the ordinary men and women of the day had little part to play in the shaping of society. Government was something 'given'.

Now, in a democracy, every citizen has some say (however small) in the politics of his country. A Christian could conceivably decide to opt out altogether, refusing to vote or in any way to accept responsibility for secular society. In that case, to be consistent, he ought also to refuse to pay income tax because this is the way in which most citizens do, in fact, incur responsibility for what government does. But unless he does opt out, a Christian is *in* politics for good or ill. In a context like South Africa he can begin to feel himself compromised simply by being a citizen. He is living in a curious half-world, where sometimes the ordinary conventions of a normal society seem to apply, and sometimes they do not. If one is a member of a university senate which is under pressure to endorse some morally objectionable government policy (perhaps in exchange for a new computer) and one is outvoted by one's colleagues, is one bound by the normal conventions of collective responsibility? If one is, is one 'responsible' for what has been done? Is one free to seize a placard and join a group of students protesting against the senate's decision? Or is resignation the only action open to one? And, if resignation also means giving up one's job, which issues are important enough to be worth sacrificing one's family future for? Each time resignation is postponed, on the ground that the issue is not important enough or that one may do more good by remaining where one still has some influence, one feels that integrity has been further compromised.

If one has to negotiate directly with government, the compromising character of this half-world becomes more obvious. One may be a member of the governing body of an institution whose property the government is proposing to expropriate. Though it is never openly stated, the reason for the expropriation is that the government is determined that no other influence than its own shall shape African education. Does one simply make an out-and-out protest against the proposal and wait for the inevitable? Or does one negotiate in the hope of gaining a few more years, or a new but remote site where the institution will be 'harmless', or a compromise solution where one's own ideas about education may survive in however diminished a form? When one decides to negotiate, one finds one has accepted the rules of the game. The mere fact of talking round a table with those who represent a different set of values *and the power to enforce them,* seems to put one in a position where it is assumed that one *shares* those values. It is like sitting down to play chess against an opponent who moves all his pieces as if he were playing draughts, and who is able to compel one to do the same. What one had thought was going to be a compromise over practical detail, turns out to be a compromise of principle if not of one's one moral integrity.

It is this perpetual sense of being compromised which makes it possible to sympathize with those who abandon the half-world and join the revolution where, at least, the issues are clear-cut.

In a real democracy most citizens are not conscious of being continually compromised in such a manner. But the Christian who feels that he has a vocation to serve society in a political career or in the public service may very well do so. His over-riding commitment cannot be to a political party, though party allegiance may be the only path to political service. Nor can it be to any class or section within the nation. It cannot even be to the nation itself, though public office will involve giving his allegiance to the nation. His one over-riding commitment will be to the values expressed in the teaching, life and death of Jesus Christ, and where there is a conflict of loyalties it is *always* his commitment to Christ which must be the more important.

Is it inevitable that there should be such a conflict of loyalties? If one were to serve the nation and the community in a spirit of pure, selfless, patriotic devotion, determined to bring Christian ideals to bear on public life, then surely there need be no conflict. Unfortunately, there seems to be some degree of truth in the popular assumption that politics is a dirty game in which one cannot preserve clean hands. There is currently considerable interest among the moral philosophers in the conflicts between public and private moral standards,[8] and the conflicts which seem to arise even when one's private moral standards are not specifically Christian. In other words it appears that ordinary decent behaviour, let alone the over-riding claim of Christ upon the Christian, is not compatible with public life. It seems to be taken for granted that the occupant of a public office simply could not behave according to the same moral standards as would be expected of him in private life. Quite different standards are held to apply. Lying, concealment, broken promises, coercion and what amounts to bribery, are thought to be politically necessary *even when they are recognized as morally unacceptable.* Public roles and offices, and the service of national institutions, are treated as though they conferred a sort of moral immunity. And that suggests that society as a whole has come to the

[8] E.g. Stuart Hampshire (ed.), *Public and Private Morality,* Cambridge University Press 1978, and cf. Sissela Bok, *Lying: Moral Choice in Public and Private Life,* Haworth Press 1978.

conclusion that it is impossible to apply normal moral standards to the affairs of politics.

One politician, David Owen, has attempted to demonstrate, in print, how he sees his Christian commitment and his party allegiance as complementing and not contradicting one another.[9] It is not a particularly profound book and it may be unfair to treat it as if it were an attempt to resolve these moral problems. But it begins, significantly, with a defence of compromise which exhibits two curious features. In his anxiety to show that compromise is better than rigid, inflexible principle, Owen seems to make compromise itself a basic moral principle. And he also fails to distinguish between compromise over policy and moral compromise. If a minister believes that arms sales are wrong, yet fails to persuade his cabinet colleagues to his point of view, he may have to compromise. Economic necessity, treaty obligations, or the need to maintain a balance of power, may compel him to allow the continuation of such sales. The best he can hope for is a compromise which moves in the right direction by reducing the volume of the sales. It is this kind of compromise which Owen is really defending. But probably even the most ardent pacifist would not be greatly upset by a compromise of that sort. He would be able to see that it was an improvement. If, however, the minister publicly denies that arms sales are taking place (when they are), there is quite a different order, a different *sense,* of compromise involved. It is not a compromise *over* policy but a compromise *of* his own integrity. It is possible to compromise between arms sales and no arms sales. There is no possible compromise, in the sense of a mid-point, *between* truth and falsehood.

Moreover, we all know from experience that it is much easier to lie a second time, and easier still the hundredth time, as one's conscience is hardened and one becomes corrupt. Motive is important, of course. A man may lie very

[9] David Owen, *Human Rights,* Jonathan Cape 1978, n.b. pp. 2 f.

reluctantly and in a good cause. But that is only part of the story. It becomes easier each time to convince oneself that the cause is good. One's reluctance becomes less of an obstacle.

At the very time when the Reith lectures were being delivered, the aftermath of the Bingham report on Rhodesian oil sanctions seemed to demonstrate the difference between public and private morality. The politicians made exculpatory statements which, since they conflict, cannot all be true. It was obvious also that some civil servants had been guilty of concealment, if not of more positively dishonest practices. What was reprehensible was not what was actually done in southern Africa. It would have been perfectly proper to argue openly that sanctions were wrong or unenforceable. But it was done dishonestly, to deceive the British public and Britain's official allies. Loyalty to the truth seems to have been over-ridden by loyalty to dubious government policy, perhaps because both major political parties were implicated and it was in no one's interest to pursue the truth.

What matters in affairs of this sort is not that a lack of integrity is contemptible or sad. It is not that once one has heard a man tell an 'official' lie, one will never quite trust even his 'private' truth. It is not even, in this context, the perversion of the human being involved or the waste of human potential. What matters, in the context of this essay, is that it is plain that politics cannot be left in the hands of the professionals, even when they are Christians. For the implication seems to be that either they will be under such pressure to compromise their integrity, in order to reach positions of influence, that they will cease to be a *Christian* or a *moral* influence, or, if they retain their integrity, that they may not be allowed to reach those positions at all.

All this may seem to reinforce Norman's argument that man is corrupt and society not worth bothering about. If the professionals are not to be trusted; if synods and assemblies act from very mixed motives; if lone protesters are often confused and frightened; would it not be better to keep out of politics altogether? There is another and possibly more optimistic view. Perhaps the function of Christianity in politics is precisely *to be uncompromising*— the salt that must not lose its savour—and a standing example to, and critique of, society—the lamp set on a lampstand.[10] This role cannot be left to the professionals, not only because they are under great pressure to compromise and will have to make painful sacrifices to retain their integrity, but because they live permanently in the half-world, where it is not easy even to be sure when one *is* compromising. So society also needs to be challenged by those who, however simple, naïve and unworldly, are able to stand apart from the practice of politics and see the issues in stark moral terms. But, because this, in turn, is a lonely and sometimes frightening role, the Church as a whole—corporately and officially—also needs to say its say.

Sin will always be present, as in every human activity. What matters, from the Christian point of view, is that it should be recognized and treated as sin, neither excused as 'professionalism' nor regarded as a cause for total despair. That is, after all, what the 'pure' gospel is all about. Provided that sin is recognized as sin, it can be confessed, repented of, forgiven and redeemed.

[10] Cf. Matthew 5:13–16.

Duncan B. Forrester

The Ecumenical Renovation of the Gospel

E. R. NORMAN's views on the origin and dissemination of contemporary Christian attitudes seem at first glance to have some plausibility; certainly they deserve closer and critical examination. He sees Christianity as having in the last twenty years become radically politicized, so that the distinctive emphases of the Gospel have been effectively abandoned in favour of a wishy-washy reflection of secular political idealism. This process is rooted in the West, where it has already enervated and all but destroyed living Christian faith; but it has been spread by expatriate clergymen and a westernized elite of church leaders, and is already showing signs of sapping the vitality of churches throughout the world. Norman depicts in his lectures a truly amazing intercontinental and ecumenical Christian consensus against his position—Roman, Anglican, Orthodox and Reformed Christian leaders in Europe, America (North and South), Africa and Asia have got it wrong; all have been beguiled by the seductions of political idealism and have forgotten what Christianity is really about—all, that is, except Norman and a few South Africans and Russian Orthodox leaders and the tiny Anglican Church in Chile (composed largely of English businessmen), who have realized that Christianity has no fundamental investment in liberty, human rights, and justice.

Dr Norman underlines that he is speaking of church *leaders*, not of the rank-and-file. The response to his lectures suggests that in Britain there may indeed be an ominous gulf between the views of leaders who have been influenced by the ecumenical movement and the man in the pew, who often enough cannot understand or accept much that comes from such a forum as the World Council of Churches. But in the Third World, we are informed with little or no supporting data, it is no different: the articulate and radical Christian leaders are not the authentic spokesmen of the oppressed, but a westernized elite voicing the prejudices imbibed in western or western-style seminaries, the very views which are at the root of the decline of Christianity in the West and which, if successful, will also undercut the flourishing Christianity of the Third World.

Conspiracy theories such as this are always intellectually titillating, and appeal strongly to those who dislike the ideas being propagated, but they often do not stand up to inspection. It is not easy to understand how ideas which amount in Norman's opinion to a radical perversion of Christian faith should be diffused so easily and take root so deeply all round the world and in the soil of virtually every Christian confession. The facts are not only capable of a different interpretation but call out for more adequate explanation. The process whereby Christian attitudes are shaped is far more complex and challenging than Norman allows, and surely in the complexities is to be seen much that is a genuinely Christian and prophetic response to the realities of the day. What if the new consensus represents a deepened understanding of the Gospel, and the recovery of a more universal and critical faith?

Norman's use of the concept of politicization deserves close examination. One may admit that there are cases where the distinctive content of Christian faith has dissolved away into secular idealism (or secular cynicism, for that matter: a possibility Norman does not consider), while rejecting his assertion that all or most contemporary

Christian involvement in politics betokens a radical compromising of Christian faith. Norman seems curiously unwilling to examine theological issues, or enquire concerning the theological roots of present-day radical or revolutionary politics, perhaps because his argument depends upon the assumption that there are no such roots. It is quite clear that the contemporary theology which accompanies and relates to the tendencies Norman deplores does not arise out of Bultmann's demythologizing or Tillich's theology. It is not the heir of the death of God theology of the 1960s, or derived from Harvey Cox's eulogy of the secular city. It is a theology of substance which calls for a critique more serious and balanced than Norman's crude sociological reductionism. Among the more prominent and influential political theologians Gollwitzer,[1] Lochman,[2] Moltmann[3] and M. M. Thomas,[4] have clearly been deeply influenced by Karl Barth; Martin Luther King[5] and Paul Lehmann[6] are indebted particularly to Reinhold Niebuhr; Gutierrez,[7]

[1] Helmut Gollwitzer, Lutheran, Professor of Systematic Theology at the Free University of Berlin. A prominent disciple of Barth's, his writings translated into English include *Unwilling Journey: A Diary from Russia* (an account of his experiences as a prisoner of war), *The Existence of God, The Rich Christians and Poor Lazarus,* and *The Christian Faith and the Marxist Criticism of Religion.*

[2] Jan Lochman, Czech Reformed theologian, formerly of the Comenius Faculty in Prague and now professor in Basel.

[3] Jurgen Moltmann, Professor of Systematic Theology at Tübingen, and author of many works, most notably *The Theology of Hope, The Crucified God* and *The Church in the Power of the Spirit.*

[4] M. M. Thomas of India was for a period Chairman of the Central Committee of the World Council of Churches. His many writings include *The Unknown Christ of the Indian Renaissance.*

[5] Martin Luther King, American Baptist leader of the civil rights movement.

[6] Paul Lehmann, Professor of Systematic Theology at Union Theological Seminary, New York, and author of *The Transfiguration of Politics,* etc.

[7] Gustavo Gutierrez, Latin American Roman Catholic, author of *A Theology of Liberation.*

Segundo[8] and Sobrino[9] are influenced by Karl Rahner and the Second Vatican Council; Bonino[10] is an evangelical Protestant. They come from various lands and a variety of denominations. They differ substantially among themselves and are not easy to lump together as a unified school of theology. But no one who has read them could fail to count them as serious theologians, struggling with the perennial problems of theology and producing results which are stimulating and raise serious questions both about Christian practice and about theological method. It is just not good enough to dismiss them in a cavalier fashion as E. R. Norman does. Curtly to assume that they are no more than pale reflections of the radical idealism of the moment is about as convincing as it would be to suggest that Barth's *Church Dogmatics* is nothing but an insipid and ephemeral reaction to Hitler. Barth's work was stimulated, it is true, by the political problem of the day—Nazism—and he saw himself as having a major responsibility for encouraging an authentic and costly Christian response to Nazism, as to other political questions. His response to Hitler involved taking theology with renewed seriousness, for only a profound and firmly rooted theology was capable of sustaining a Christian orientation. To indulge in the kind of crude sociological reductionism characteristic of the Reith Lectures is to fail to take theology— or indeed systematic thought of any kind —seriously.

Having said that, one may not unilluminatingly enquire how the Reith Lectures themselves fare when subjected to a similar type of analysis to that directed by Norman at the

[8] Juan Luis Segundo, Roman Catholic director of the Peter Faber Pastoral Centre in Montevideo and author of *The Liberation of Theology.*

[9] Jan Sobrino, Roman Catholic, San Salvador, author of *Christology at the Crossroads.*

[10] Jose Miguez Bonino of the Higher Evangelical Institute for Theological Studies in Buenos Aires and author of *Revolutionary Theology Comes of Age* and *Christians and Marxists.*

so-called 'politicization of Christianity'. He implies that his position is founded on some perennially valid understanding of the essence of Christianity. His version of Christianity may seem plausible within the confines of an Oxbridge ivory tower, but to the Third World Christian it looks singularly like a radically Europeanized version of the Gospel, uncritically cultivated in the schools and singularly oblivious to the suffering and the questions of the world. His unease at the 'politicization of Christianity', his inability to enter sympathetically into the yearnings and the theologizing of Third World Christians, and his constant assertion that their thought is simply the echo of western ideologies which he finds unacceptable betray the typical western difficulty in adapting to a world that is no longer Eurocentric, no longer dominated, politically and otherwise, by the West. The fact that there is so little theological argument in his lectures, that he hardly troubles to explain or defend his own version of Christianity, makes one suspect that he believes it to be self-authenticating. But Third World Christians and those in the rest of the world who have been influenced by ecumenical contacts do not see this position as self-evident at all. They are entitled to better than they receive at the hands of the Reith Lecturer; they surely deserve to be listened to critically but modestly by western Christians. The spirits are to be tested, it is true, but one gets the impression that Norman has never been really open to the possibility that in contemporary Christianity there may be a deepening and a broadening in the understanding of the Gospel rather than a simple perversion, that amid the complexities and uncertainties and conflicts of today the Spirit may be leading the Church into truth, and enabling a renewed apprehension of fundamentals of the Faith.

Dr Norman is well aware of the seductive power of contemporary ideologies. He has argued that it is hard to see anything that is distinctively Christian in Christian social thinking. He presses this point too hard, for although Christianity has always found it necessary to relate closely to, and often borrow from, secular or non-Christian ideologies and ethical systems, it has also shown discrimination in the ideological views which may be espoused, and those which must be rejected, often radically transforming concepts and patterns of practice to make them fit for Christian use. Ideology may be seductive, but it is also inevitable, and Norman's position is as ideologically conditioned as any. His version of Christianity is very close to that which was exported at the beginning of the modern missionary movement; the changes to which he objects evolved largely as a result of the new, open and equal ecumenical dialogue between Christians in many lands which has now become possible with the erosion of the relationships of dominance and dependence characteristic of colonialism. Such relationships obstruct understanding and lead to lopsided views, in religion as in other matters. But the new situation in which Christians from many contexts speak to each other on a basis of equality and challenge each other to re-examine the Gospel and the limitations and possibilities which flow from their varying culturally conditioned perspectives is found deeply threatening by those who used to dominate but no longer can do so. From this flows the patronizing, even badgering tone so characteristic of the Reith Lectures: Third World Christians have got it all wrong; they have been led up the garden path by politicizing leaders and missionaries. Consequently their theology and their practice need not be examined modestly and seriously, but are ruled out of court by the arrogant assumption that western Christians (or some of them) have got all the answers right already. One point of view is absolutized, and alternatives are brashly dismissed.

It is not only in theology and religious matters that similar issues arise. Early social anthropology, for instance, not infrequently produced vast stamp collections of the quaint beliefs and behaviour of 'primitive peoples' based on the assumption of the absolute superiority of western culture. The resulting information was often interesting, but superficial and inadequately interpreted, and certainly was not gathered in the hope that the western anthropologist might learn about himself and adopt a critical stance towards his own society and its values in the light of his understanding of other societies. But gradually as the anthropologists' method became participant observation, they learned that deeper understanding of another society was possible only by what a remarkable anthropologist couple called 'the leisurely way of friendship'.[11] Furthermore, it was found that this kind of anthropology was not only more illuminating in itself but inevitably involved a new assessment of oneself and one's own society. Increasingly it became impossible to absolutize one's own point of view. A similar transformation took place in development studies, discussed by Robert Moore in his essay. The effort to ape the western path to development has come to be seen as often destructive because it paid such scant regard to the cultural, ideological, religious and economic factors which provided the resources for change in each particular context. In anthropology and development studies unfounded absolutism propagated by the politically dominant obstructed the enlargement of understanding. The same has been true in theology; and here too there are now new possibilities of the enlargement of understanding if we take seriously, as Norman does not, the new ecumenical forum in which Christians from widely different backgrounds may share their insights and their understandings of the implications of Christian faith on a basis of equality.

All this has implications for our understanding of the

[11] C. and W. Wiser, *Behind Mud Walls,* Berkeley and Los Angeles 1967, p. xiii.

nature of theology. Norman is right to suspect a theology
which merely reflects the fashions of the age or the
dominant ideology in a culture. Theology, like all sciences, seeks a truth which is universal and relevant to all
situations; it cannot rest content with total relativity. It
believes that there is a fundamental connection between
knowing, loving and doing. The serious theologian does
not hold that he already possesses the truth, but is always
eager to test and enlarge his grasp on the truth. He therefore constantly measures the adequacy of his understanding against new situations and differing theologies,
expecting his own views to be challenged, enlarged and
modified. He is, or ought to be, particularly open to criticism, especially when this comes from within the
household of faith. He finds in himself, of course,
resistance to this openness because it involves putting so
much at risk; but if he recoils from the encounter he loses
his integrity as a theologian. It is not easy for the European theologian to listen to Christians from other
lands speaking to him of the limitations of theological understanding imposed on him by the place where
he stands socially, politically and culturally, by the specifically western assumptions which have been smuggled into
his thought, by the ways in which his theology may be used
to dominate and to legitimate structures of injustice. But he
must listen, and listen humbly and sensitively, because he is
a Christian and because he is a theologian. Would that
there had been more of this humble listening evidenced in
the Reith Lectures!

There are interesting parallels to be found in the social
sciences to this search for universality. Karl Marx, having
developed a theory of social change based upon western
data, could not rest content without examining in detail a
wide range of past societies and asking how far his theory
remained valid in such diverse cultural settings as those of
India and China. And Max Weber, venturing hypotheses

on the relation of religion and economic development based on an examination of the origins of capitalism in the reformation period, started immediately a gigantic and never completed study of other cultures to test his theory and expand its scope. If theology is to be more than a reflection of the spirit of the age it must be no less serious in seeking deeper and more universal understanding of truth, testing its conclusions and hypotheses in relation to practice in different settings, and radically open to advance through dialogue with others.

It is instructive to look at particular instances in some detail to see whether the process of politicization is as recent or as deleterious as Norman thinks, and whether his theory of the development and diffusion of such ideas and patterns of behaviour is convincing. Consider, for instance, Protestant missions in India.[12] The early missionaries in the eighteenth century and the first part of the nineteenth century took with them a theology of which we may presume E. R. Norman would highly approve. They were on the whole evangelical pietists, convinced that their task was the proclamation to individuals of a Gospel which was concerned with eternal salvation rather than social reform. They felt their own social and political attitudes to be of little importance; certainly they were not to be propagated among the Indians. Political and temporal affairs they could safely leave to the government and pursue their own proper business of saving souls. Their preaching had effect; in number of converts not as much as they had hoped, although converts they had. The content of their preaching began to change in the early nineteenth century, in certain important particulars becoming more political. They had encountered in caste a social system which was a major barrier to their evangelism. Caste offended their Christian moral sense by obstructing acts of common humanity be-

[12] This is documented in detail in my forthcoming book, *Caste and Christianity*.

tween those of different caste. It divided and weakened society, it seemed an integral part of Hinduism and, most serious of all, it denied the dignity and equality of man by teaching that some were inherently and irremediably polluting. The missionaries concluded that if caste distinctions were to be countenanced within the Church it would become a visible denial of the Gospel it preached. They regarded the issue of caste as being no less crucial than had been the question of overcoming the division between Jew and Gentile in the early Church. Accordingly they insisted that converts renounce caste on baptism, and express their new faith by publicly eating with fellow-Christians of different caste origin, thus definitively separating themselves from caste society by breaking its central rules. Eucharistic commensalism became for them a direct and practical implication of Christian faith. As a result conversions from the higher castes were few—the sacrifice of social status and the breach with Hindu society were demands too strict for most. But converts came in large numbers from the ranks of the untouchables and others of low caste. Missionaries found themselves involved in a wide range of endeavours to improve the lot of their poverty-stricken and despised converts, and also increasingly turned to political action to protect them against oppression and injustice. Nor was it only a matter of the internal life of the Church and the defence and uplift of converts—quickly missionaries came to see caste as something to be attacked and questioned by every means in their power wherever it was found.

Here, clearly, is a process of politicization going on. The Gospel the missionaries preached has a strong egalitarian emphasis, far more explicit and central than that found contemporaneously in the home churches from which the missionaries came, and it involves a social and political commitment quite alien to the missionaries' earlier views and often, to begin with, uncongenial to the sending missionary societies. This egalitarianism did not reflect the accepted position of the home churches and in many ways it made the missionaries' task in India more difficult and less rewarding than it might otherwise have been. The secular utilitarians also disliked caste, and some of their reasons were the same as those of the missionaries; but they did nothing to combat caste. The missionaries acted, with passion, to express their opposition to caste. Liberal idealism, in this case at least, looks like a pale reflection of Christian social commitment. And it is often that way today, despite Norman's simplistic assertions to the contrary. What factors shaped the missionaries' assessment of caste? There were, of course, many; but prominent among them must be this: the situation in India as they found it had forced them to a reconsideration of the Gospel, and in it they found that which made imperative a costly onslaught on caste and a new conviction of the Christian significance of social and political action. In transfer and in application the understanding of the Gospel was changed; yet certainly not in such a way as to dissolve its content into secular idealism.

That is not the end of this particular story. The new awareness of egalitarian implications in the Gospel suggested that the western churches had allowed a vital part of their understanding of the Gospel to be compromised in such a way that they could not see its implications for themselves. The Indian converts, having gladly made the costly break with caste, began to ask about the bearing of the Gospel on the missionaries, on their churches, and on the society from which they came and which they regarded so uncritically. If it were indeed important that Christians from every caste should gladly eat together how, the converts enquired, can one defend the prohibition of eucharistic commensalism between the various imported denominations? Are denominational differences, Christianly considered, of a totally other kind from caste distinctions? And what about the racialist arrogance shown by some missionaries and so many of the missionaries' fellow-countrymen? Surely the Gospel which had been shown to be incompatible with caste was no less antagonistic to racialism. And what of western class? Different it might be from caste in numerous respects, but were these so substantial that the Gospel could live at peace with a society in which the luxury of a few was based upon the poverty and degradation of many? The missionaries did not like these questions, and most of them for long resisted the application to themselves of the principles they had preached. The historian can see quite clearly how in the dialogue and interaction between cultures the understanding of the Gospel and its implications develops. The process may not inappropriately be labelled politicization, but is certainly not properly understood as a conspiracy or confidence trick. It is not an enervation but a renovation of the Gospel. And certainly it is no slavish, easy adaptation to the mood of the age.

I have considered this case in some detail because it is an excellent paradigm of the process E. R. Norman dismisses so glibly. From pietist origins, engagement with social and political issues follows naturally and inevitably, without in any way losing contact with a living Christian spirituality. Indeed the understanding of the Gospel is enlarged and purified. Such a process takes place especially when there is real meeting of Christians from varying cultural and denominational contexts. It is often painful, but it is a growing pain. By the distorting application of a simplistic sociological reductionism E. R. Norman encourages British Christians to return to their complacent slumbers, unwilling to embrace the challenges and opportunities presented by the new ecumenism, and unable to see that the Spirit is at work and the devil does not have it all his own way. Kwame Nkrumah's slogan, 'Seek ye first the political kingdom', was engraved on his statue which stood in Accra while he was in power. Norman is right that this is heresy;

only it is not the motto of those he castigates. They take seriously what he does not: that disciples are bidden to seek first the kingdom of God, and accordingly cannot, in Barth's words, be 'indifferent or neutral towards the political structures of this world which are so clearly related to [the Church's] own mission'.[13]

[13] Karl Barth, *Against the Stream.* London 1954, p. 22.

Robert Moore

Christianity and
Human Rights

I

ONE major problem in responding to Norman is recognizing the world he inhabits. It is a world threatened by a
Marxist conspiracy and 'Marxist' is identified with
phenomena as varied as the regimes of Eastern Europe and
the policies of Salvador Allende. A tangle of unexamined
assumptions are carried in the simple assertion of an identifiable threat. In the Third World there are conspiracies in
which the normally conservative masses are being stirred
up by western or western-trained intellectuals. This assertion reminds me of Patrick Wall's profoundly irrelevant
observation upon the film *Last Grave in Dimbaza*, namely
that the 'kettle drums' must have been added to the sound
track by 'black intellectuals in Paris'. There are, of course,
conspiracies in history, but one does not need a conspiracy
theory of history in order to explain events in the world in
the 1970s. Conspiracy theories usually serve to explain to
members of an establishment why previously right-
thinking and respectable people are challenging a perfectly
agreeable *status quo*.

How do the churches behave in Norman's world? This is
a hard question to answer because he selects certain aspects
of the work of the World Council of Churches to stand for
the churches. The WCC seems to have decided and committed itself unanimously upon a wide range of social and
political issues. Other contributors to this volume can
describe more accurately the lack of consensus in the WCC

and its agencies. I can only say that the words and deeds of the wcc have had a minimal effect upon the average Christian, except perhaps the setting up of the fund to combat racism. Incidentally, this observation damages Norman's contention that ideas are sustained by elites. Norman likes the elites (except when they suborn peasants) and especially those near the centre of things who are therefore 'effective or accurate in their political judgments' (p. 604). What Norman plainly does not like—and has to explain by reference to conspiracies—are 'effective or accurate' political judgements made away from the centres of power.

The wcc has apparently fallen victim to the *zeitgeist* of left-wing collectivism. But the spirit of the 1970s has been corporatist not collectivist. We have seen the destruction of parliamentary socialism in Europe and the subversion of left-of-centre regimes outside Europe. In these introductory and negative comments it is not necessary to dwell upon political analysis but it would be easy to document the assault upon the living standards and quality of life of the British working class since 1970.[1] But one would need to set this in the context of changes in industry, the occupational structure and of changing class alliances. Importantly, however, Norman contrasts the threat of collectivism with the liberal values of bourgeois democracy. This is a specious contrast; most liberal freedoms were revolutionary freedoms and were fought for and won at great personal cost. The right of association is one such right, freedom of speech and the right to trial by an unpacked jury of one's peers are others, all are now threatened and in need of vigorous defence not against the left but from right-thinking people like the Attorney-General, Mrs Thatcher and Sir Robert Mark.

[1] For good guides to sources of information on this topic, see two booklets whose style and tone may not please every reader—but which gives the information nonetheless—Reports No. 13 and 18 from Counter Information Services, *Cutting the Welfare State* and *Paying for the Crisis.*

Problems of sociology should not, however, obscure the extent to which Norman either fails to support his own arguments with evidence, or merely descends to the absurd. For example: he asserts (*The Listener,* (1978) p. 632) that when the WCC published *How to File Complaints of Human Right Violations* the human rights movement was rapidly becoming political. The volume he cites is as political as the telephone directory, and about as interesting to the general reader. It is a simple account of how to use the legally established international machinery for realizing the human rights established by international agreements. The WCC published this presumably because no commercial publisher could profit from doing so and few governments would offer a guide on how to take themselves to court. Norman should approve of the opportunities the book affords the common man to defend private property or private education against the 'collectivist' state. The act of enabling people to achieve what is granted them by the legitimate national and international legal system is hardly political in Norman's sense. Norman makes too much of the title of a book and too little of its content, just as he sets too much store by the labels people appropriate to themselves rather than studying their actions and the consequences of their actions.

II

As far as it goes Norman's sociology of knowledge is correct. It would be remarkable if secular and religious thought did not respond to the circumstances of their time. As circumstances change so do the ways in which we understand the world—although there is no simple formula by which changes in one may be related to the other. We may also learn by experience in unchanging circumstances. But I find myself at one with Norman in believing that religious as opposed to secular thought is concerned with universal, timeless and unchanging verities. Religion and society are in tension. According to Christian eschatology a certain future state of mankind is inevitable, yet I must participate in working for that inevitable outcome (a paradox not unknown within Marxism). The hectic conflicts of today's political issues contrast sharply with the surrender of the Cross. The notion of redemption—renewal, salvation, rebirth—contrasts with continuous political compromise and self-deception. A gospel of hope is a mystery that I really do only see through a glass darkly in a world heading for political or ecological catastrophe. The hardest truth to bear is the knowledge that one must love one's enemies and recognize in the most inhuman despot a man for whom Christ died.

The tension between the eternal and the temporal exists at the level of ideas and as a matter of experience. This is unavoidable because we are in the world and have no other space within which to understand and express belief and hope. It is reassuring to discover the secular challenge of religion in the Old Testament as a feature of the experience of Israel. In the New Testament Jesus begins His ministry with a reference to the fulfilling of the jubilee teaching (Luke 4:16–21) and later said that the quality of our devotion to God is to be measured by the quality of our service to 'one of the least of these' (Matt 25:31–46).

III

If the world changes then our Christian response must change unless we seek complete withdrawal and no longer even try to do good. The Gospel offers us no ready-made outfit of responses suitable for all seasons. Even if the world changed very little we might still expect to learn from experience and adapt accordingly. Thus Norman has underestimated the extent to which the thinking of the WCC (his example) reflects real changes in the world rather than attempts to follow intellectual fads and political fashions. Let me first give an example of growth without much change in the world: when I was a student many members of SCM were becoming involved in (or founding) social service organizations to serve the needy in their local community. True Christian love and charity was expressed in youthful and selfless energy and idealism. My fellow students served one particular street, taking meals to the aged, painting poor people's flats and just sitting and talking to the lonely and rejected. In 1964 there was a rent strike in the street and the road was barricaded against the bailiffs—with much publicity. During the dispute my friends discovered that when they painted flats the tenants were evicted so that the accommodation could be let at a higher rent; that the local authority had failed to meet its obligations to the tenants and that many of the older people and larger families had long been entitled to rehousing. They also discovered that the agent for the worst rent-racking landlord was a pillar of the local establishment, an alderman and member of the University Council. For some of the students involved this was a turning point. They recognized the extent to which their charity had been expressed in a form which aided the exploiters and the negligent and helped their victims unnecessarily to endure the intolerable conditions of the street. None of them ceased good works but many of them extended their activities to the more overtly political in order to strike at the root causes of the conditions they had sought to ameliorate. This seems to me to have been a growth, a maturing in the practice of the faith, arising from experience. The changes in political outlook of the late 1960s was an outgrowth from such experiences and not a response to intellectual fashions. If Marxism became a fad in this period it was because it offered an explanation and a remedy to conditions that were recognized in the practice of Christian charity. The church had little to offer at the time. In the street, the parish priest—an evangelical—refused to baptize children because they were the children of prostitutes. He did more to radicalize my high-church friends than an army of Marxist conspirators could have ever hoped to achieve.

An autobiographical comment may underline both the extent to which an individual may grow in response to the world and the ambiguity and uncertainty of the growth. In the late 1950s I was an officer in the Navy and as a Christian accepted that living by the sword I must be prepared to die by it (Matt 26:52). The advent of nuclear weapons with their promise of massive and indiscriminate killing and genetic disaster presented an unavoidable moral challenge. After solitary soul-searching and long debates with pacifists and non-pacifists I resigned my commission. My objections to nuclear killing logically led me to pacifism and so I found myself a Christian pacifist. My response to the changing nature of warfare changed the course of my life. Today wars of liberation in Africa and elsewhere present another moral challenge. I still aspire to be a Christian pacifist but, full of misgivings and with great anxiety, I find myself at least a passive supporter of these wars. The bloody, and I hope brief, struggles of oppressed people seem preferable to interminable oppression. But I am not the helpless victim of some *zeitgeist* (or a fickle radical who changes last year's CND badge for this year's 'Free Zimbabwe'). I am no more a victim than others who opposed unilateral nuclear disarmament in the 1950s and 1960s and now find themselves opposed to all violence in Africa. Like them, and no doubt many members of the WCC, I am anxious and uncertain even now. I believe also that faith, the church, the sacraments enable one to transcend—but not avoid—anxiety and uncertainty, and gives one hope to continue in spite of error and guilt. One is continually and painfully reborn and redeemed.

To return to Norman's thesis: if then we eliminate the

zietgeist or the idea of political fashion or radical chic from our explanation and adopt a more solidly based sociology of knowledge we have to ask: What have been the changes in the world that have led the WCC to adopt an apparently radical political stance? Crucially and to argue on Norman's ground we need to ask why attitudes have become implicitly critical of capitalism and why race and human rights have become such central issues. One can only begin to sketch an answer in a short essay.

In the post-war period Christians were concerned, in a traditional way, with problems of hunger and disease in the under-developed countries. As ex-colonies achieved political autonomy the western churches quite properly handed over church government to local Christians too. As colonies passed from tutelage to autonomy in the political and ecclesiastical spheres Christians sought to help the 'newly emergent' nations to help themselves. Alongside relief work there was an urge to give financial and technical aid so that underdeveloped countries could develop independently. The ex-colonies were seen as being in a state of underdevelopment but none the less upon the road to development. With capital, technical inputs and goodwill from the industrial nations they would 'take off' and achieve a developed state.

The expectations were not fulfilled and understanding the failure opened many eyes to the realities of international relations. The underdeveloped countries were not simply behind us on the road to progress, they had been actively underdeveloped in the colonial period. The transition to formal political autonomy revealed continuing economic dependence. The economies of the independent countries—often based on a range of products limited by the colonial regime—were geared to western markets rather than local needs and the price of cocoa, rubber, sugar, minerals and other primary products were controlled by western commodity exchanges. Even the attempted

Green Revolution was abortive because it tied farmers to western technology, and to western petro-chemical companies for fuel and fertilizers. The Revolution meant debt for many, and those who partially succeeded did so at the expense of expropriated peasants as landlords extended their holdings, enhanced their political power and foreclosed on indebted tenants.

Large tracts of the Third World continued to be turned to produce cash crops for export. Self-sufficient peasants were turned off the land to make way for agribusiness and food had to be imported to meet local needs. Niger, for example, became a net importer of food in the 1960s and today parts of Senegal are still going out of peasant production to grow ground nuts for the U.S.A. Some of the most depressing documents to pass across my desk are research reports of thousands of peasants in various parts of the world being moved to poorer land or forced to join the shanty-town dwellers, so that their traditional land may be used by big business or for government irrigation schemes that will serve foreign business. Whatever we hoped for the underdeveloped countries it is plain that many corporations had quite different plans for them and the means for putting the plans into effect.

Much aid was, and is, in the form of trade credit, obliging developing countries to buy western manufactures. How much cash has flowed to Latin America through the Alliance for Progress? The dollars were made available for purchases in the U.S.A. Money that did go to Latin America under the terms of the Alliance had to go to private enterprise, thus precluding public works in building roads or houses. Furthermore, the Alliance precluded radical land and tax reform and was seen by President Kennedy as allowing only reforms that would 'preserve the fabric' of the societies concerned. In other words, the main beneficiaries were American corporations and the marginal benefits to some Latin Americans depended entirely upon their compliance with U.S. policy. Only recently we had a powerful image of the 'fabric' of Latin American society in a TV film *Children of Peru*; in the mountains people living at or just below survival level, on the coast Peru's rich harvest of fish being canned for export.

More recently the activities of industrial corporations in Third World countries compel us to believe that they see the Third World as a pool of cheap and compliant workers who may be used to undermine the economic and political position of workers in the 'advanced' countries. Multinationals enter Third World countries on their own terms because of the demand for employment and create unemployment in Europe and the U.S.A. This role of the peoples of the Third World is underlined by the presence of 11 million of them in the EEC, working in services, deskilled or low status jobs in manufacturing, or in tasks traditionally undertaken by dependent workers. The condition of these immigrants became a matter of concern for the European churches, who not only tried to meet some of their needs and remedy their deprivations but to understand why they were here at all.

These generalizations refer to specific conditions of mankind to which Christians felt compelled to address themselves in their love and charity. When Christians asked about the root causes of deprivation, poverty, hunger, oppression, their *simpliste,* liberal onwards-and-upwards view of development as a natural process was distinctly challenged. They found the rich and the powerful operated in a world-wide range of options in the pursuit of profit and that profitability was more important than human need and was, indeed, unable, by its own logic, to meet need. Want and oppression were often the conditions of profitability. When local people recognized this and sought to alter their circumstances by political action the ruling élites found ready allies in the governments of the industrial powers. *Here* are the western-trained élites[2]: men in power equating development and modernity with westernization and western life-style for themselves and despising their own people.

Western Christians learnt this through involvement, through experience either in work overseas or on behalf of underdeveloped countries. Many Third World Christians knew all along but were patient in waiting for us to discover what they already knew. As we were learning so real changes were taking place; capitalism itself is very progressive according to its own logic and this results in new forms and changing relationships throughout the world.

At home circumstances have changed too. Most notably the more advanced industrial methods for the pursuit of profit entail a substantial decline in the number of jobs, more repetitive and boring work for those who are employed and harder work to keep their jobs. Men now serve machines rather than machines serving men. The profit created does not go into creating new jobs or a more caring society but into potentially more profitable speculative activity, into investment overseas, dividends or share issues and conspicuous consumption. Meanwhile in Britain the welfare state is being dismantled before having a chance to approach adequacy and private enterprise is stepping in to provide pensions, health care and education for those who can afford it (or whose employers can afford it for them). New vistas of 'two nations' open before us. It is as hard for me to characterize three decades of political and economic change as it is for Norman to characterize the church in six lectures. Both of us tend to create caricatures. None the less, what I have outlined is not a fevered Marxist analysis but facts salient in the experience of those who have tried to do good works and to exercise Christian charity towards their fellow men at home and overseas.

[2] See Orlando Lekelier "Chile: Economic 'freedom' and political repression" *Race and Class* Vol XVII No 3 pp 247–260.

That progress was to be achieved through the agreement of men of goodwill and a new society built by harnessing scientific knowledge in the service of man were beliefs widely held after the Second World War. At the extreme it seemed that Utopia was possible, at a minimum that every man might expect to live a healthy life with enough to eat. The bright visions have faded, we find ourselves subject to institutions that can deliver neither peace nor enough to eat. It is important to note in this context when Norman disparages 'collectivism' that the vast majority of the world's people have only their collective strength with which to defend or improve their circumstances or with which to resist the powers and principalities that make their lives burdensome. An analysis of recent history, or more importantly, firsthand experience of the events that comprise it, may seem radical or left wing to Norman but this is a question of viewpoint, or interest. If you are one of the disinherited or 'the wretched of the earth' you do not need a Marxist or a western-trained intellectual to explain your history to you—the explanation is all too obvious.

The issues and the analyses have been forced upon Christians, history was not of their choosing. The only escape is in indifference to the condition of mankind in the world, and this seems to entail a defective kind of theology. It entails rejecting the concern for the widow, the orphan, the poor and the hungry which was part of God's demand upon Israel and of Jesus's teaching. Most of us in the West find it very hard to come to terms with selling all we have and giving to the poor; but surely none of us believes the Gospel invites us to live off the poor? Yet this is what we do in the western world.

IV

Considerations such as these have made race and South Africa central to the concern of the WCC and western

Christians in general. South Africa combines totalitarianism with ruthless economic exploitation and it is a society where political domination and economic power is co-terminous with racial divisions. In the racial conflict we see images of man formulated in the popular mind, where wives and children can be called 'superfluous appendages'. Adherence to such views disfigures the humanity of those who hold them. South Africa therefore combines all the worst elements that we find distributed amongst the social and political systems of the world; it is a peculiarly offensive distillation of all our worst evils. This resonates with opinions in the U.K., partly because of our historical responsibility for establishing the regime and partly because of our continued support of the regime in the world political arena. We are also the direct economic beneficiaries of the oppression, so to our other responses is added guilt. Our reactions cannot be disinterested. The churches have looked beyond the justifications and rationalizations offered by the regime (including the fallacious notion of 'separate development') to the fruits of the regime's policies. What they have seen are not social arrangements of a kind about which gentlemen might disagree, but evil. And they have listened to the cry of the oppressed. To respond to that cry is not to fall in with the *zeitgeist*.

The race question has become important in Europe also because members of ethnic and national minorities play a crucial role in the maintenance of western European industry and services whilst occupying positions of political subordination. They are found also to be concentrated in the worst paid jobs and the worst housing throughout Europe. The immigrants are here 'voluntarily' in only the most notional sense. The majority come from areas made poor by their economic relationship to Europe and have been actively recruited by European employers with offers of work and a good life in a land of plenty. In Britain successive governments have allowed blacks none the less to become scapegoats for the failure of social policies. If we are to believe the Crossman diaries, Harold Wilson went further and accepted racism as a datum from which to develop immigration and race policies. How should a Christian respond to the adoption of a debasing image of man as a basis for policy? Policy is now rooted in the notion of irredeemable human degeneracy with which one can only compromise. Blacks themselves have become direct victims of oppressive policies; the immigration laws themselves—as I described at length in 1975[3]—have been used to oppress as much as control. Most seriously, there has been an assault upon the family, with the threat or the reality of the prolonged separation of spouses or parents and children used both as a deterrent to immigration and settlement and as a means of reducing the totals in the appropriate colums of the immigration statistics. Families have been broken up permanently and men and women driven to suicide by these practices. British wives have no statutory right to have non-U.K. husbands living with them in the U.K. although their husbands could live with them anywhere else in the EEC. The sanctity of the family has always been central to Christian moral teaching and Christ himself loved family life and little children. I am amazed at the tolerance shown by the churches to the state's attitude to the family—I cannot believe that they would so easily tolerate equivalent treatment of native families. Race relations or human rights are not therefore abstract or ideological issues but concrete matters affecting identifiable people in the U.K. in a way that compels or should compel Christians to action and to oppose the state.

The effects of the immigration laws (or immigration colour bar) go further and stigmatize all black people as a potential threat who are only here by lack of foresight. In

[3] *Slamming the Door: the Administration of Immigration Control* (with Tina Wallace), Martin Robertson 1975.

the mid 1960s senior policemen predicted that police involvement in immigration control would have a corrupting effect upon policing and this has proved to be an 'effective and accurate' political judgement. The powers given to the police and other authorities by the 1971 Immigration Act lead to the disruption of domestic tranquillity and the violation of the home by raiding policemen. Blacks are under suspicion all the time, no longer fully free citizens, but likely to be asked for papers at any time or held in custody for lengthy periods without charge. And why should they not be thought to be potential illegal immigrants, for who would not break the law to join their wives and children?

The declaratory function of the legislation and the circumstances of its enactment reduce inhibitions in the arbitrary use of power that might be felt by those in authority and makes it easy to act in a discriminatory way. The climate of mistrust and suspicion is spread further as the state demands that schools, hospitals, National Insurance and Supplementary Benefits officials check upon non-British and non-whites with whom they come into official contact. If this were not enough, the development of the immigration colour bar has encouraged racists to campaign for more restrictions and to back these demands violently—thereby apparently confirming Mr Wilson's original assumption. These are realities: I doubt if Norman has experienced them. For blacks—many born here—Britain is a house of bondage.

I had intended to make a discussion of the idea of the house of bondage in the Jews' sense of history and in their understanding of their destiny central to my reply to Norman on human rights. It now comes briefly and at the end because it seemed necessary to establish the empirical base of the churches' thinking in order to counter Norman's view of fads, fashions and conspiracies. My ending will be a beginning of a critique of the churches in Britain in which I suggest that the concerns Norman believes the WCC to pursue world-wide are badly neglected by the churches in Europe and in the U.K. especially. Britain may not be a house of bondage for blacks only.

The race issue in Britain has an existential nastiness of its own but it also combines with other issues to create in Britain what has been called a 'moral panic'.[4] Race, muggings, violence, terrorism, drugs, permissiveness, pornography, strikes, punk rock, political dissent are but some of the issues which headline and leader writers take together to suggest that the whole fabric of our society is under threat. There is an 'enemy within' as well as a world Marxist conspiracy. The separate issues are not treated separately and their extent, causes and remedy carefully examined; rather the criminal statistics are abused and single incidents amplified and the constant assertion that we are under threat alarms, and disarms the critical faculties. It induces a fear in which demands for the removal of traditional safeguards upon the individual's freedom are agreed too readily and hastily and action is taken by the state which would be unthinkable in calmer times. The passage of the Prevention of Terrorism Act in the aftermath of the Birmingham bombings is one good example, the 1968 Commonwealth Immigration Act passed in a period of induced panic, is another. Meanwhile the agencies of the state, especially the police, the army and the intelligence services have been gaining experience of covert and overt 'people control' in dealing with Northern Ireland, immigration and preparations for hijacking. Modern techniques give them the tools to store and collate vast quantities of data about the public. The state has become more interested in the company that we keep, the organizations that we belong

---

[4] The term was used by S. Cohen in *Moral Panics and Folk Devils* (MacGibbon and Kee 1972) but in the present context developed by S. Hall *et al* in *Policing the Crisis* (Macmillan 1978). See especially chapters 1–3 and 7–9.

to and even the books we read. Political trials under the Official Secrets Act and the Conspiracy Laws have increased and the U.K. has ceased to be a safe haven for political refugees. It is a simple next step, and one that most highly elaborated security establishments take, to provide justifications for the provisions either by the security forces themselves provoking violent or illegal acts or by providing culprits through perjury. We have probably not yet taken this step in any decisive way. Nor do we have trial without jury like Northern Ireland—but the jury system is under attack from the police. The facilities exist to operate a *berufsverbot* in either a covert or overt way—can we be sure that public opinion will not be moved to the point where such a policy would be implemented? Existing legislation makes it possible to be held without charge for three days (the police want longer) and in the case of immigration appeals to be tried without hearing the case against one's self. The notion of innocent until proved guilty is under increasing pressure. None of these developments and threats seems to have been seriously considered by the U.K. churches. Yet the churches have a good record in opposing slavery and child labour (even though Wilberforce *supported* the latter); they have a good record also in making statements on freedoms threatened overseas, in the Soviet Union, South Africa and elsewhere. In my one fairly marginal involvement with the churches in Europe I have experienced the agonizing over responses to terrorism, anxiety about Uganda, Zaire and Cambodia and the west's role in arming the worst oppressors whilst making civil rights an 'issue' in international relations. There is a strange silence on domestic affairs by the U.K. churches who may have fallen victim to our little local moral panic (which I hope will not become the spirit of the age).

The gospel tells us not to panic but to live in hope and to believe that our redemption has already begun. The Bible tells us that we should see justice done (Ezekiel 4, Micah 3,

Romans 1–6), that judges are not to be bribed (or panicked), that the poor, needy, widowed, sick and imprisoned are cared for. Throughout the Old Testament Israel had to cope with the shadow of a house of bondage, whether it was the actual threat of a new captivity or of a Jerusalem-based despotic regime undermining the freedom and independence of the rural life of the tribal federation. Always they were told to avoid bondage and to see justice done—I often wonder whether it was the church or the state who first relegated Amos and Hosea to 'minor' prophetic status!

Norman lives in a world in which oppression is common and he can find cases very near home. But let us assume for a moment that the church should not be involved in politics. Equally hypothetically: if Norman meets an oppressor— whether it be Idi Amin Dada or a local rent-racking landloard—what Gospel message would Norman like to give them? Would not the news that their redemption was begun and is continuing alter the pattern of their lives if it was taken to heart? Is it unreasonable to assume that oppression might stop—in which case Norman will have intervened in the (secular) interests of the oppressed? If oppression does not cease will Norman not feel Christian-duty bound to remind the unrepentant oppressor of God's promises to those who 'trample the head of the poor into the dust of the earth' (Amos 2:7)?

I suppose Norman may have a concept of the 'Christian oppressor'. If he could expound the notion clearly we could all be saved a lot of bother in committees and conferences. One might also tell the oppressed to bear oppression and suffer in silence in hope of a better world hereafter. This has been tried before, not altogether unsuccessfully. I do believe that Christians should learn to bear pain and oppression calmly in faith, and that the worst tyrant is held in the palm of God's hand. But what kind of man would Norman think he was who told people to suffer avoidable pain, hunger, death or degradation in silence—especially when he can help them avoid it, or at least cease to derive direct benefit? We know too little from his lectures of Norman's theology of man.

Let us return finally not to the victims, about whom we may have romantic and unrealistic ideas from time to time. What about the violators of man and men who treat others as merely the means to their own ends? It seems to me that the words of judgement spoken to all of us apply unmistakably to them—as does the Gospel of redemption—and both are political in their consequences.

Paradoxically it may be that the radicalism that Norman finds in the churches as represented by the wcc is not an attempt to stir up the poor to reckless acts of resistance or to violent revolution. Maybe the churches are at last speaking God's word to a badly neglected minority—the powerful, the ruthless, the oppressors of His poor. If they, in turn, find the words disturbing and unsettling, perhaps they are listening.

Daniel Jenkins
Faith and Politics in Britain Today

I

ATTACKS on the alleged 'politicization' of the Christian faith by churches are becoming increasingly frequent. That by Dr Edward Norman is only the most elaborate and the most widely publicized. Their trouble is that they themselves are often made from positions which are highly 'politicized' in their turn. They also appear to lack historical perspective. After all, the story of the relation between Christian faith and political activity is long and complex and a great deal of work has been done over the last generation in sorting out the issues involved, not least under the auspices of the now much-criticized World Council of Churches. No one in this century can have shown a more acute awareness of the distinction between Christian faith and political activity, nor more sureness of touch in dealing with delicate political issues, than the first General Secretary of the World Council, Dr W. A. Visser 't Hooft.

It is a good question, to which Dr Norman, as a historian, might profitably have addressed himself, as to why that awareness and sureness of touch were so quickly lost in the sixties, not least in the World Council itself, but the fact that it existed does suggest that this matter is likely to be most helpfully discussed in a larger context than that of present controversies. In the light of Christian thinking over a longer period than, say, the last ten years, it should be possible to reach at least a measure of widespread agreement about a Christian approach to political activity which should make mutual understanding easier. Nothing is more unhelpful, or more culpable in the present situation, than that Christians should dissipate their energies in unnecessary controversy with one another.

First, it would be widely agreed among Christians that their faith is not primarily about politics nor about trying to build an earthly social order, however desirable it might be. It is about God and His covenant with his people as it has been made known in the life, death and triumph over death of Jesus Christ. His kingdom is not of this world, even though life in this world must be lived in the light and by the power of that kingdom through his Spirit.

Secondly, it would also be agreed that Christian faith calls all human motives into question. No human being has the right to call humanity 'rubbish' but, in the presence of God, we all know ourselves as radically sinful. In the period of the Enlightenment, and of the theological Liberalism which was influenced by it, some Christian spokesmen were disposed to minimize the extent of our estrangement from God, and of the damage done by it. It was surely in this period, running for well over a century, rather than only in the last decade, that Christian thinking was most affected by 'secular' values. Part of the achievement of the outstanding theologians of the first half of this century was to provide a critique of those values through a new insight into the sovereignty of God. Reinhold Niebuhr's work was particularly illuminating in exposing the ambiguity attaching to all human institutions and the need for vigilance on the part of those who were deeply convinced of the righteousness of their cause and of themselves as its defenders.

Thirdly, it is undeniable that Christians are especially vulnerable to this kind of self-righteousness and only too quick to identify the will of God with furthering their own 'righteous cause'. History abundantly demonstrates that this is not a habit peculiar to politically left-wing clerics in the sixties and seventies of this century. It has happened throughout the ages and Christians have been much more disposed to fall into it with reference to the established authorities of the communities in which they lived than to movements for revolution and reform. After all, one of the traditional objections of Protestant Dissenters to the Established Church of England, in which Dr Norman himself holds a responsible position, is that it has accepted the deliberate institutionalizing of such an identification.

Fourthly, sober Christians would agree that their faith gives them no automatic possession of any greater purity of motive, insight or competence in the sphere of politics than anyone else. This is particularly true of professional Christian spokesmen, such as clergymen, whose vocation carries peculiar dangers in this sphere of which they do well to be aware. What they should have, however, is a measure of detachment from immediate political concerns which could be helpful to their fellow Christians who are more directly involved in politics. This should both make them constantly aware of the relativity of all political judgements and causes and of the strength of the temptation of politicians to absolutize them. The characteristic function of the pulpit in relation to politics should be to raise questions and to promote self-criticism rather than to do what politicians of every kind eagerly look for, which is to provide support for their own cause.

If Christians can agree about these propositions, they can do much to deliver political activity from the demons which always hover around it and which can so quickly make it totalitarian. They can encourage patience, sobriety and realism about what can and cannot be achieved by political means. Yet this is obviously very far from saying that politics should have no interest for the Christian and that political activity should be eschewed. Apart from anything else, it is unavoidable in one form or another for

anyone who lives in society. Even a decision not to participate has political repercussions and, therefore, cannot be
responsibly taken without a consideration of political factors.

Over and above that, Christians in the world are meant
to be active. All are meant to wait on God. For some this
may mean that the major part of their time is spent in
prayer, contemplation and study but, even for them, waiting on God is a matter of giving priority of attention in the
midst of the distractions of this world to discovering his will.
It is not one of being simply passive in the midst of events.
When his will becomes clear, it involves fresh action. This
usually means changes in relationship, attempts to influence the attitudes and behaviour of others and a new distribution of human resources. In other words, it involves
action which has many points of similarity to action in the
sphere we normally label political.

Politics, we are often reminded, is about power. So also,
we are not so often reminded, is the Christian faith. It is
true that its relation to power is very different from that
which comes naturally to us all as citizens of the world but
the fact that they have this element of power in common
means that the relation between the Christian faith and
politics is both particularly close and particularly easy to
mishandle. Nowhere is it more important than here that we
should be aware of what we are doing and why.

Jesus began his ministry as someone endowed with quite
exceptional power. The story of his temptation, which is
placed as a kind of preface to his ministry in Matthew's
Gospel, is best read as a summary of his long struggle to
isolate and expose the false uses to which his great power
might be put in the attempt to fulfil his vocation. As a result
of this struggle, he insists that this power can be used only
by his taking the form of a servant. It turned out that human
nature, especially in its organized social forms, refused to
accept that power and did its best to neutralize it.

The only way in which he was able to fulfil his vocation was through voluntarily embracing the powerlessness of the Cross. It was this alone which made available a fresh access of power in the Spirit, coming from outside the normal resources of human nature.

The fact that things happened in this way drives home two truths of the greatest consequence for the Christian understanding of power. The first is that, although this power of the Spirit is essentially positive, it remains that of one who allowed himself to be crucified, unaided by any human power, one whose own followers forsook him and fled. This means that *all* human power is corrupt and stands under the judgement of God. This refers not only to political power but also to what we call 'spiritual' power. The New Testament, after all, does not make a sharp distinction between the two. It is not only the activities of politicians and the direct servants of the state which come under judgement but also those of pastors and teachers and parents and marriage partners. The more personal and intimate the power involved, the more directly they do so. All power is corrupt and, therefore, all power needs critical scrutiny and careful checking by others than those who exercise it.

The second truth follows from this. It is never enough for those who believe that their cause is righteous to conclude that this conviction legitimizes their use of power. This is why no Christian can give unconditional support to any cause, nation, party or institution, however admirable its aims and compassionate its spirit and however dedicated the service it inspires. Christians can be as loyal and committed as anyone else on many levels but they can never allow their loyalty and commitment to make them forget the element of ambiguity in even the most righteous cause. They will also particularly remember that when a cause triumphs and those who serve it are flushed with new-won power, then its righteousness is at its most precarious. If there is anything that recent experience in politics confirms, both in Britain and in several countries which have recently achieved political independence, it is that no self-righteousness is more intractable than that of those whose cause has just triumphed, since their former righteousness provides an irresistible justification in their own eyes for the promotion of new unrighteousness to their own advantage.

Power relations are so closely interwoven with the very substance of Christian living as it seeks to transform this sinful world that merely to complain of the 'politicization' of Christianity is naïve. To the extent that it is alive at all, Christian faith must always be in process of 'politicization', with all the consequences of corruption which that entails. Our only hope is frankly to recognize this fact and to draw on the ample resources of Christian insight for self and mutual criticism, which make possible again the 're-Christianization' of our relationships.

Unless this radical critique of all relationships which have a power-factor involved in them takes place, politics in the more limited and customary sense of the struggle between organized groups for power in the public domain is unlikely to have much health. Churches which, in an attempt to 'keep their hands clean', try to neglect the political dimension and concentrate only on what they call 'spiritual' things are both deceiving themselves and failing in their public duty. Christians cannot escape from the problems inherent in living in this world by creating for themselves some kind of ecclesiastical buffer-state whose symbols and procedures claim a unique purity because they refer only to ecclesiastical affairs. No matter how much it is dressed up, that buffer-state remains simply one part of this sinful world, having its full share of the possibilities of corruption inherent in all human activity. Observation also suggests that it also contains its full share of ordinary politics, something distinguished from their more overt forms only by being less inhibited by moral scruple and civilized convention.

That this happens should not be surprising, because those who make such buffer-states their home misunderstand the relation between God's kingdom and this world or, to use another New Testament term, between the age to come and this present age. It is an obvious travesty of the apostolic community's strong awareness of the imminence of the fulfilment of the kingdom to think of it in terms of 'pie in the sky when you die'. Difficult as it may be for us to enter into their kind of eschatological expectation, it clearly arose out their knowledge of a purpose other and greater than ordinary human purposes, and one which was moving towards resolution in its own time, not ours. It gave them a vision of the future which, so far from distracting them from the present, quickened their sense of the significance of what they should be doing here and now. Their order of priorities was changed but the grip of moral realities upon them was strengthened.

More than that, what happened when their awareness of the imminence of the End diminished is revealing. They did not conclude, as some have supposed, that their expectation had simply been proved mistaken and that they must now proceed on the assumption that life would now go on very much as before. On the contrary, they remained convinced that it had been right and that the insight given them in the intensity of their initial experience should still govern their actions as they awaited their Lord's pleasure. The goal set before them still stood and their chief aim remained that of pressing forward towards it. They returned to the old image of this life as a pilgrimage. As pilgrims, their steps were always to be directed by what lay at the end of the journey. Whatever delights and dangers met them on the way, they were not to allow them to set the limit of their horizon and thus to misdirect them. This world was not their home and to be trapped again into supposing that it was, would only mean that they had fallen back into the bondage from which they had been delivered at great cost. Yet the fact remained that it was through this world and no other that they had to pass and it was this world which was illuminated by the light of the world to come. They saw that the condition of effective action in this world was faithfulness to the vision which they had received of life in the world to come.

The implication of this for us could not be more direct. The Christian community should certainly refuse to allow 'the world to write the agenda for the Church', to use the misleading phrase which had some currency in World Council circles until recently. Even if those who coined it wanted to react against the undue ecclesiastical self-preoccupation against which I also have just been objecting, it still implies an uncritical acceptance of what those who are most vocal in the world think important. The world's priorities are rarely those of the kingdom and, anyway, it would be difficult to find an agreed agenda. It is the world to come which writes the agenda for the church. Yet it remains an agenda for her action in this world and the teaching of Jesus, especially that with an explicit eschatological reference, says that that agenda will take account of very down-to-earth matters, such as feeding the hungry and clothing the naked (Matt 25:31–46). Christian other-worldliness is not something separate from 'holy worldliness' but provides it with its inspiration and its objectives.

II

Any observation about community life in Britain today made in the light of the ideas outlined in the first part of this paper must be tentative and limited in scope. Christian spokesmen who are not involved from day to day in public politics should be able to see issues in a longer perspective than most practical politicians. This predisposes them to deal in generalities, and as such could be helpful, but only if those generalities are related as closely as possible to practicalities and if the spokesmen firmly resist their own temptation to exploit political commentary in order to demonstrate their own moral superiority.

It is appropriate, therefore, that the first observation which suggests itself from a Christian point of view about our present situation should be deflationary in relation to moral pretentiousness in this field. The British people over the last generation have come to expect too much from political action and from the legislation produced as a result of such action. Whether or not British Christianity has become excessively political, it is undeniable that British public life as a whole has. Apart from the single contentious issue of the social tolerance of forms of sexual behaviour previously considered to be dangerously deviant, ours is as unpermissive a society as this country has ever known. The rule of the saints was a very loose-reined affair compared to the present rule of the fusspots. The individual cannot put up a garden shed or fix a bottle-top or weigh an egg without becoming enmeshed in a network of regulations, and any small group has to watch its step lest it offend a government board appointed for attitude surveillance. Ever since the Second World War, the state has got into the habit of taking too much upon itself. Consequently, society has come to expect more of its politicians than they can possibly deliver, and in their anxiety to please they vainly try to meet these expectations. This has long been obvious in economic affairs but is becoming increasingly clear in other spheres as well, especially with reference to education and social welfare. It is no longer entirely a joke to say that now the government has appointed a minister to deal with problems made by the weather, it will not be long before it is held responsible for the movement of the elements.

This point is not made in any political party spirit. The

extension of state activity over the last generation arose as the expression of a greater sense of equality and social solidarity than our society had known in pre-war days and as an attempt to improve the quality of life for everybody. As we shall see, it is vital that these social gains should be conserved. Our argument is not the same as the familiar plea for 'individualism' or what is called 'private enterprise' as against 'socialism'. All these phrases have now become ideological, that is, coloured by the interests of particular groups, and fresh content badly needs to be given to what was positive in the ideas originally expressed by these tired slogans. Our point is made in relation to all public politics, whatever their label. The process now seems almost out of control. Even those politicians who set out to reduce the area of government activity quickly find themselves in a situation where they have to create new organs of government to do even that, so that their last state is worse than their first. The chief objection to the EEC and to plans for devolution in Scotland and Wales is that, whatever merits they may have on other levels, they will inevitably mean more jobs for politicians and the extension of the area of government control, with the inevitable related expansion of bureaucracy.

When things have reached this stage, there is only one way in which the trend can be reversed without social breakdown. Initiatives must be taken to revive real private enterprise. I need hardly emphasize again that this is sharply to be distinguished from the ideology which goes by that name, that of people in business who want the government to be organized in their interest rather than in that of the rest of the community. By 'real private enterprise' I mean the determination of individuals and groups to take initiatives of their own volition and at their own charges, resolutely declining state patronage or subsidy. This, after all, is the classic way in which reform and social development used to take place in this country. In the past, the state has been accustomed to take over, often with the goodwill of those concerned, a service whose utility has been demonstrated by private initiative. In the future, it may be necessary for private initiative to demonstrate that certain services are best provided independently of the state. Without such initiatives, our state is likely to be organized more and more in the interests of those who direct, administer and are employed by it rather than for the sake of the community as a whole.

For all its present weakness, British society is still not without examples of such initiatives. One of the most obvious has been the growth of such agencies as Christian Aid and similar bodies. No one can argue that such voluntary agencies could, of themselves, do much to narrow the gap between rich and poor countries, but their spirit and their methods, linked as they are with the long and honourable traditions of the Christian missionary societies, sometimes enable what help they have to offer to be more effective than that provided through official channels.

Similarly, Christians should have a special interest in initiatives to make people's lives simpler on the material level and in promoting self-reliance, if not necessarily self-sufficiency. 'Small is beautiful' and the emphasis on intermediate technology were themselves the product of a Christian initiative. More needs to be done along these lines, especially in relation to larger communal units and to urban and suburban conditions. The smaller and more committed nature of many church groups as compared with earlier times should make it possible for some of them to undertake experiments along these lines themselves.

The same is true of issues raised by the fact that the proportion of the population which is elderly is on the increase. Churches of all institutions should have ideas about realizing the potentialities of old age and maintaining dignity and independence in doing so. More controversially, some would argue that the need for fresh initiatives in providing *inexpensive* forms of private education in places where the dominance of particular educational dogma or professional vested interest make the state's provision unacceptable is also becoming more obvious. I have made some suggestions in my book on *The British: their identity and their religion* about initiatives which might be taken, independently of politics, over relations between the English, the Scots and the Welsh. Churches should also remember that they are still important organized social groups in the community and that this is a counter-weight to the incipient totalitarianism of the state. In their planning for the future, they should not lose sight of the need to maintain the institutional toughness and resilience necessary for this function.

The ability to take or participate in initiatives of this kind is one of the surest indices of Christian vitality. This does not, of course, alter the facts that politics are still with us, that they are very important and that they encompass activities in which Christians are deeply involved. Contrary to popular impression, the proportion of leading politicians who are either themselves active churchmen or who belong to families with unusually strong Christian connections can rarely have been higher than in the last decade. They have ground for complaint that they have not received the amount of discriminating support and pastoral help from the rest of the Christian community, and especially its clerics, which they might reasonably have expected. In so far as the recent British Council of Churches Report *Britain Today and Tomorrow* was representative of prevailing opinion in the churches, they do not appear to have much which is distinctive to offer in their corporate capacity about policies and programmes. But there is a treasury of wisdom from the past, including the quite recent past, which could be of immense practical value to politicians and administrators—wisdom about motivation and relationships, about ambition and egotism and loyalty and compromise, about institutions and about power, its corruption and its redemption, about the vanity of many human wishes and yet the reality of solid achievement when worked for with patience and foresight and perseverance. Politicians, carrying such heavy burdens as they are required to at the behest of a lazy and capricious public, badly need candid friends with no axe to grind who can give them criticism and encouragement. Christian ministers exist to be such friends to Christian politicians.

I should be the first to insist that in doing this, it is imperative that they retain their own independence. They cannot avoid being concerned with the political sphere, and they have an obligation to be of what help they can to those engaged within it, but they must always see it in the setting of the coming kingdom. Whatever pressures may be brought to bear upon them from the world of politics, their primary concern will continue to be firmly theological.

It is particularly important to remember this at present. All the signs are that we are at the beginning of a major conservative revival in Britain, conservative in relation to personal morality and the environment and the heritage of the past as well as to economics and politics. Several of the leaders of this revival are intelligent and articulate Christians, and some aspects of it can be warmly welcomed from any Christian point of view. This very fact makes it all the more important that it should not be greeted with simple, undiscriminating enthusiasm by the Christian community. If anything can be confidently predicted, it is that the number of ecclesiastical hangers-on who will jump on to a conservative band-waggon once it starts to roll will far exceed any who have jumped on to a radical one. A trendiness of the Right is no less of a deflection from the way of a pilgrim than one of the Left. It could be argued that it is more, since it will have a stronger inclination to stay among those already favoured by inheritance and fortune and therefore all the more reluctant to take the risks of moving forward.

For a conservative revival to be truly discriminating, it will see that part of what most needs conserving is the best of our quite recent past. A Christian perspective on history should warn us that nothing is easier than to detect the faults of our immediate predecessors and to undervalue their achievements, while it is natural to idealize the more remote past. A great deal of improvement took place in the internal life of Britain between 1940 and about 1960. The wave of idealism, social solidarity and compassion which produced those improvements seems now to have spent itself and, with the passing of time, their inevitable inadequacies have become more obvious. Our public services need overhaul, abuses need to be corrected and over-optimistic schemes to be revised. Conservatives are probably right to argue against their political opponents that more of what we already have, which is no longer working very well, will probably only intensify our present malaise, but the very concern for quality which they advocate should make them see that this is too good an achievement to throw away and that, in the current mean-spirited and querulous mood of the nation, we would only replace it with something worse. Christian spokesmen who understand the dialectical relation between the conservative and radical tendencies in society, and the fact that both are easily corruptible, will strive to retain their independence of judgement as much when one tendency is in the ascendant as when the other is.

I am well aware that observations of this kind are considered tame and uninspiring by some ardent Christians. They prefer to see their Christian political mission more dramatically, in terms of demonstrations and 'crusades'. They might reflect that demonstrations rarely amount to more than just that and that crusades have a way of turning out very differently from the original intention. This country has become old and tired. It will not be reborn except in the slow, quiet and painful way in which new birth takes place. That is unlikely to happen in the first instance in the political sphere and we probably need to look elsewhere for the first shoots of new life. Meanwhile, as far as politics is concerned, we do well to be modest in our pretensions and try to be as quietly constructive as we can in helping those who bear the heaviest burdens.

James Mark

Politics and the Religious Dimension

My reaction to Dr Norman's lectures was a mixed one. I recognized the force of what he had to say about the political emphasis of a good deal of contemporary Christian thought, both in the West and the Third World—an emphasis which sometimes (notably in some 'Black theology') reaches the point of interpreting the Gospel purely in political terms. It is right to point out that, to say the least, there is more to the Gospel than this. On the other hand it seems to me unsatisfactory that, when we have a series of Reith Lectures devoted to a Christian theme, it should consist largely of someone speaking of what he doesn't like. It makes for thin fare, and gives a negative impression of what Christians concern themselves with. Moreover, although he lands some shrewd blows, I find his political analysis oversimplified to the point of distortion, and his view of the Gospel ethereal to the point of having little to do with life together and even less with life in society. These are criticisms which other contributors develop more fully. Nevertheless, when one examines the implications of what he says, one realizes that he is raising some issues of the first importance about Christian concern with political affairs. And this remains true even though he doesn't, for the most part, bring them out clearly or adequately himself.

The most fundamental of these, no doubt, is the fact that in *some* sense, of course, the Gospel does transcend political argument. If we feel that he has not expressed this transcendence adequately, how can it be more adequately expressed? But then, what do we make of his argument that, in the light of this transcendence, all 'Christian' political ideals may be equally sincere but are equally invalid: that Nyerere's Christian socialism is 'no more "Christian" in this sense than Franco's Fascist Spain'? Given that some of us, at least, are political animals, what does this imply about the way in which we ought to address ourselves to politics. If we dislike his relativist scepticism, how do we refute it? What, indeed, are the implications of the evident fact that Christians whom we must regard as no more or no less sincere, intelligent and unselfish in their attitudes, disagree in their views on any given political question? But they do not seem, in our own society, to be equally articulate. Why is it that the dominant tone of political and social comment in the British churches is liberal or rather further left? What has happened to Christian conservatism, and is it not a serious criticism of our Christian political thought that we hear so little of it? An alliance of conservative interests does, after all, make up one of the two largest parties in the state.

I shall start with the last of these questions, for two reasons. It does mean that we begin, as Norman did, from our present situation, and this may help to earth any comment on the more general questions. And it does draw attention to one of the more striking features of the way in which most Christians (or most articulate ones) seem to view it. I shall limit myself to Christian opinion in this country; that in the Third World (which comprises, in any case, a diversity of countries) is something very different, with its own complex roots, and has been discussed by other contributors. In my view the predominant tone in the discussion of social and political affairs in the British churches, and in their public pronouncements, is liberal-to-left. The recent studies of the British Council of Churches, *Britain Today and Tomorrow,*[1] provide striking evidence of this.

[1] See Trevor Beeson's book under this title (Collins 1978).

The fringe of clergy and laity who show greater sympathy with Marxism is small. I would describe them as *marxisants* rather than Marxists, since few Christians in this country seem to have failed to recognize, whatever their sympathy with Marxist economic and social analysis and criticism, that dialectical materialism is ultimately irreconcilable with a Christian view of life, and that Marxist theory, therefore, continues to reject religion in general and Christianity in particular. But why should this liberal tone predominate? Norman argues that it is because Christianity has lost its distinctive faith and has substituted secular ideals: even that those radical theologians who want to reconstruct our theology provide most of the 'advocates of social activism', though one does not recognize such figures as Wiles, Nineham, Houlden, Cupitt and Hick among them. There is truth in the contention that, when theologians find it possible to say less about the hereafter, they may put more emphasis on understanding and living out Christian faith in the world we know. But the roots of whatever change has occurred in Christian political and social teaching lie in the changes that have taken place in our society rather than in our understanding of Christian doctrine.

Conservative political philosophy has rested, traditionally,on limited expectations of what men can be expected to achieve in society. It has regarded them as weak, selfish creatures who can only co-operate, at best, imperfectly. That co-operation can easily subside into chaos without the disciplines of custom and an established order which, however faulty and unjust, does at least provide stability. But ideally, of course, custom and order should help to produce an organic society, in which each has his place and finds his satisfaction in filling it, and doing his duty in the state to which God has called him. Hobbes emphasizes the negative aspects: authority is necessary, however imperfect, so that selfish and wicked humanity may be kept in order. At much the same time the Stuarts were enunciating the romantic (and for English ears exotic) doctrine of the divine right of kings. But what man can do in society and what society can do for him are always limited. His real concern is as a sinner in the sight of God. Nor were these assumptions limited to the political philosophers of Toryism. Others who could assert a claim to share political power may have had more optimistic views of how it could be used, and different ideas as to how it should be shared; but, apart from the radical fringe which showed itself mainly at times of unrest, the common assumption was that the sphere of political action was limited and that society itself was unlikely radically to change. It was this, after all, that made the English Civil War so shocking an event to the rest of Europe, and so unable to maintain itself after the death of the man who consummated it. It may be (and always has been) argued that views such as these suit very well the interests of those people who are favoured by the existing order, and can be used to justify keeping the less fortunate in their places, and this is true. Any political view expresses an interest. But this is not to say that it is devoid of truth. Men are imperfect. The prospect of civil war and unrest was never far away. There are things that matter more than what men do together in society. It was considerations like these that made a man like Dr Johnson—no aristocrat or friend of aristocrats—such a convinced Tory, while asserting that he would not give half a crown to live under one form of government than another. Johnson illustrates another aspect of this view of society. The welfare of what we would now call the under-privileged was a matter for private charity. Johnson gave up to three-quarters of his income to it.

One has only to rehearse these assumptions to recognize how vastly they have changed. This has happened in the economic and social spheres by the sheer ability to create wealth, which was being discovered towards the end of Dr Johnson's day and has grown with increasing speed ever since. It has transformed our world. We expect economic growth; we do not regard our material prospects as limited to those that we know. We accept the change that economic growth involves: the social fluidity, the dissolution of communities, the *provisionality* of our political and social arrangements, and therefore the provisionality of the authority by which we are governed. We find ourselves, moreover, in a world which has grown smaller because the forms of economic organization demand a whole world in which to operate, and because the technology which supports it brings us all closer together.

Such changes naturally have profound effects on what can be done to promote human welfare. Prospects of betterment appear; there is increasing wealth to be distributed, and the structure of society becomes looser, so that change is more easily possible. Above all it comes to be seen that something can be *done* about ancient poverty and ancient wrongs. If economic problems can be solved why not these also? Justice can be done at last. The pathetic peasants' revolts of the past are replaced by the power of the organized labour which is essential to the economic activity. A philosophy of social change develops, which sees the triumph of the proletariat as inevitable, because its justice is undeniable. Wealth can be used to promote social welfare, and political power can become the instrument for that promotion.

It is not surprising that there should have been a shift to the Left in the predominant mood of political and social thought, since this is where the impulse towards change has always been. Traditional Tory philosophy has, indeed, virtually disappeared; Conservative thinkers, like others concerned with politics, have had to develop their thought on different assumptions. There has been hardly any disposition to question the need to create wealth; the argument has concentrated on how it can most effectively be created; what is to be done to control the power that economic organization creates; and how the wealth created is to be distributed. But, whatever the change in our political assumptions, the differences between Right and Left on those issues dear to liberals, and on which Norman is so sceptical, are by no means clearcut. It would be hard to say, for example, whether Left or Right has been, in practice, more sensitive to questions of human rights, or to the claims of the Third World to a larger share of the economic wealth that the world can produce.

Whatever the ambiguities of the political parties it is clear that articulate opinion, at least in the churches, has become increasingly preoccupied with the changes that can made for the better, both here and abroad; with the injustices to be remedied; the rights to be assured; the sharing of the increased wealth of the world and of the resources to create it. Nor is this surprising. How can Christians reject the claims of the neighbour, now that they seem to be answerable—or at least to demand answers—not merely in individual but in social terms? It is this challenge to which the churches have responded. They have been franker, more emphatic and wider in their horizons than the spokesmen of the political parties, since they have not had to trim in order to conform to the demands of political tactics and electoral appeal—notably in their concern for the Third World. They may, as Norman suggests, have been naïve and ill-informed about the political complexities. But there is no mistaking the predominant tone, however one may criticize the way in which Norman may describe it, or the perspective of Christian faith in which he places it.

His criticism is that the Gospel cannot be used to justify such views, and that the spokesmen who put them forward may even substitute them for it. There is at least sufficient force in that criticism to make it necessary to ask a number of questions. The first of these is whether it is justifiable to assume that what has happened to our society in the last two hundred years or so, and is happening still with increasing speed has rendered the earlier traditional wisdom out of date. Does man's vastly increased power to exploit nature mean that he no longer needs to regard himself as a created being, responsible in some sense for a world that he did not make? Has our vastly increased power to ameliorate the human lot increased in any sense the perfectibility of man? Has it ceased to be true that he is selfish and that therefore any form of society which he can devise will be imperfect? Questions like these do not, in any sense, render the concerns of what one may call Christian social activism at all invalid. They do suggest that we should see those concerns in a certain perspective. Our world has changed; our powers are enormously increased; and our choices are, for that reason, more difficult. But nothing has changed, of course, in man's situation before God, though we may express it in different terms. No social, political or economic concern, however urgent, however deeply felt, can be allowed to obscure that truth, or the truth that no action that we can envisage will bring about the Kingdom. In that sense we may agree with Norman that the Gospel transcends the life that we know; the point at issue is the way in which it interpenetrates it.

A second group of questions arises when we consider the particular issues that we have to consider and the choices that we have to make as to what we support and what we oppose. Some are relatively simple. Thus, in spite of Norman's scepticism ('Human rights become the means by which Christians express their endorsement of the political values of their own societies'), few of us would argue that the physical maltreatment of human beings or the denial of liberty to them are defensible, and when such issues come up we do not find it difficult to make up our minds. If Russian Orthodox Christians take a different view (of cases arising in Communist countries) we cannot agree with them, though we may be grateful for being reminded that Christians are not proof against prejudice. As we move along the spectrum the issues becomes more difficult: the principles harder to express in terms of policies. We may agree that South Africa is an unjust society, in the sharing of economic opportunities and benefits among the population and the degree of liberty allowed to the non-White members of it. But the choice of means to bring about a more just one, their practicability and their effects—let alone the question of the relative claims of the white South Africans whose home the country is—are notoriously difficult and contentious. We may agree that the poorer countries should have a larger share of the world's wealth, but are we to put the emphasis on increasing the size of the cake to be shared, or in sharing more fairly a cake that may be smaller because we are consuming our resources too quickly? But most of us are probably more sharply aware of the problems of equity which arise over social and economic policy in this country. This is an aspect of the churches' concern on which Norman did not comment, since he was discussing only the alleged export of ideas by western Christianity. I need not refer to these problems in detail, since we are all familiar with them; they have to do with the relative priority to be given to the creation of wealth, its distribution, and the proportion of our resources that we should devote to publicly-financed welfare. Men of comparable intelligence and goodwill differ over these issues. Christians, equally well-informed and sincere, can be found advocating very different policies.

Norman does not probe into either group of questions; that is why I suggested at the outset that the implications of what he has to say are more important than the text itself. To consider them might lead to scepticism or to the kind of ambiguous attitude that he appears to advocate: Christians have to involve themselves in politics, but shouldn't expect it to do any good. To consider these questions might lead us to believe that in most situations there is no clear choice that a Christian should adopt, and that, in any case, the Kingdom lies beyond us. It leads me, rather, to conclude that choices, the policies to which they lead and the value-judgments which underlie them have to be argued about, by Christians among others. The argument is meaningful because none of us has the whole truth, and it is usually wrong to put forward one view as alone having merit. But just because human knowledge and understanding are limited, and human beings are selfish and prejudiced we need a religious dimension which is not, indeed, to be identified with any particular set of political convictions, but to remind us of the perspective within which we must see all such convictions. It is something that we are in danger of losing, both because human powers have increased so vastly, and because the prospects may seem so great while, at the same time, there is so much to be done and, at last, the resources seem to be available to do it.

What does such a religious dimension mean? I have little space to discuss it in detail, but in any case it is not something that can be clearly and comprehensively set out. At most one can suggest only a few indications towards something that has to be worked out by many people in many situations. It cannot, first of all, mean simply going back to the past. We need, indeed, to remember that, although we can see more of the world and make use of its resources more effectively, the mysteries remain. There is no less reason to think of ourselves as standing before a God to whom we may be drawn, but whom we cannot ultimately understand. But we cannot speak in good faith without recognizing what has happened to our situation, our possibilities and, indeed, what we can and cannot claim to know and say. The increase in our knowledge has increased our agnosticism. The religious dimension is still there; but we cannot *understand* it in terms as simple as those of our forefathers, though their language may still speak to us.

Any religious dimension must be relevant to the whole of

life, so that there can be no separate theology of politics or economics (let alone of 'liberation'); nor is theology Black or White. But there are certain themes which may be useful in provoking the right kinds of attention. One such theme is that of creation: a theme that we need to think about afresh, now that we are tempted to think of man himself as creator, and as capable of understanding the process of creation. Another is the stewardship of resources: how they are to be valued and how used. A third is that of community, and the rights and responsibilities of its members: a community which can now only be thought of as embracing the whole world. The exploration of what can usefully be said about such themes can best be pursued with a minimum of abstract generalization and a maximum of reference to the situations in which the concepts become relevant. Such exploration will reveal tensions and differences among Christians. There will be differences over the ways of achieving agreed objectives. Above all, in any Christian perspective, there will always be the gulf between the possible objectives of politics (and all that politics embraces) and the Kingdom, which is the distinctive goal of Christian faith.

For all these reasons there can never be specific 'Christian answers' to particular problems or a specific 'Christian line' on matters of public policy. What the acceptance of a religious dimension means is that we should never lose sight of certain fundamental questions which are not often raised when decisions are discussed and taken. There are such questions as that of man's position in the created world: the use and sharing of its resources. How much have we, and what are the claims to it? There is the question of the possibilities and limits of corporate action. What can be achieved and what cannot; what is likely to go wrong and how can we do the best that seems possible when we do not simply adopt the rule of from each according to his capacity and to each according to his need? There is the question of my own good faith and that of my interlocutor in the debate between us. Why does each of us advocate what we do? And if this is regarded simply as a matter of honesty and sincerity. it becomes a religious one for the Christian, who tries to see himself as Christ sees him. There is, finally, the question of the purpose of it all. To what ends are our political and economic decisions addressed, and how relevant are they to a Christian view of the end of man? To consider specific matters with such questions in our minds, and to examine the facts and the possibilities as honestly as we can in the light of them, ought to promote a greater degree of consensus as to what should be done than we command at present. But the differences will persist, because we all speak from different situations; we are not, as Simone Weil said we should be, rooted in the absence of a place. We have, in the end, to fight for the causes that seem to us to be justified—to fight as hard we can, but remembering that we do not have the whole truth and that our motives will always be mixed. We need the religious dimension, not merely to remind us of our common assumptions, as Christians, about the nature and destiny of man, but to inspire us with the common charity that must transcend our differences, as they are transcended in the Kingdom.

> These men and those who opposed them
> And those whom they opposed
> Accept the constitution of silence
> And are folded in a single party.[2]

Norman has done well to remind us that faith transcends politics; that is all too easy to identify faith with particular political doctrines or causes; and that such doctrines and causes are always stated with varying degrees of prejudice, ignorance, and impurity of motive.

[2] T. S. Eliot, 'Little Gidding'.

He is right to remind us that man's destiny is not worked out ultimately through political structures and programmes. We may add that it can be desperately difficult to judge what we are to do, in the light of faith, and to live with the results. But he has been led by his dislike of what he sees to establish a gap between the life of faith and the life of political action which does justice to neither. Bonhoeffer, who became involved in political action of the most demanding kind, left us with the question how, in his 'world come of age', Christ could then be 'no longer an object of religion, but something quite different, really Lord of the world'. But ought there to be a difference between the two?

John Kent

A Christian Humanist Replies to Edward Norman

To believe in progress does not mean believing that any progress has yet been made. That would be no real act of belief.
Kafka, *Collected Aphorisms*

DR EDWARD NORMAN'S aim, in his recent Reith Lectures, and in his major book, *Church and Society in England 1770–1970,* which provides much of the evidence on which the position of the Reith Lectures rests, is to criticize the intellectual development of the world Church, and especially of the Church of England, since the eighteenth century. He does not complain that the clergy have ceased to think: in a way, he would prefer them not to think, but to revel in unconditional loyalty to an inherited Christian gospel. His real complaint is that they too easily believe that they are thinking, and thinking theologically, when they are repeating either the bourgeois liberal, or secular humanist, or Marxist-Leninist slogans of their particular class and generation.

This is no new idea. It has long been assumed, especially by Marxist historians, that the clergy propagate the morality and political opinions of the ruling class, to which they hope that they will be admitted. But the accepted internal propaganda version of English Church history asserts that there were, nevertheless, always a few men of conscience and 'prophetic' insight who managed to free themselves sufficiently from their environment to advocate more radical, far-sighted views, from the Victorian 'Christian socialists' like F. D. Maurice, to the late twentieth-century 'liberation theologians'.

Both in *Church and Society,* and in the Reith Lectures, Dr Norman has rejected this picture. On the one hand, he denies that some of the most prominent Christian socialist prophets were actually socialist at all. F. D. Maurice, for example, was 'in plain language, a Tory paternalist with the unusual desire to theorize his acceptance of the traditional obligation to help the poor' (*Church and Society,* p. 172). As for the pompous Bishop B. F. Westcott, founder in 1889 of the Christian Social Union, he 'was not a socialist at all; he was a Chamberlain-style Liberal, whose strong sense of compassion for the working-man released itself in the assemblage of an intellectual apparatus to criticize the unpleasing consequences of what he took to be Political Economy' (ibid., p. 181). The social ideas of such theologians, whether they were old-fashioned advocates of what they mistakenly took to be Christian socialism, or modern contenders for the ordination of women as priests in the Anglican Church, were simply reflections of their own class consciousness. Radical clergymen did not actually have radical ideas of their own (according to Norman); they just borrowed them from other, often non-Christian, sections of the intellectual milieu which they frequented. 'The social attitudes of the Church', he wrote, 'have derived from the surrounding intellectual and political culture and not, as churchmen always seem to assume, from theological learning' (ibid., p. 10).

It is by no means as Dr Norman claims, that Maurice's social theology did not derive from his theological position. It would be difficult to show that Maurice's platonic belief in Christ as the animating and reconciling principle of the whole social and physical creation was no more than a reflection of his class-position, or that his soft-centred, utopian Christian socialism was no more than an ineffective Tory protest against the kind of liberal *laissez-faire* economics still canvassed in the late 1970s by Margaret Thatcher. On the last page of *Church and Society* Norman, having granted that some religio-political ideas might be valid (after all, he needs some kind of positive religious reference to give weight to his own political pessimism) still insisted that 'it is a lack of awareness by Church thinkers themselves of just how crucial class reference is . . . which makes the Church's approach to social problems sometimes appear so unreal' (ibid., p. 473). His conclusion (like that contained in the last of the Reith Lectures) is much milder than the polemic which precedes it, and seems milder still if one thinks, not of 'church thinkers' in the void, but of Coleridge, Maurice, Westcott or William Temple in their specific historical situations. They all believed that Christianity was offering men very little if it had no available model of a just society, and they were not necessarily just the puppets of their class-consciousness if they said so. They also knew in practice the truth of Kafka's aphorism, that to believe in progress does not mean believing that any progress has yet been made. If their approach to social problems sometimes seemed unreal, this was not because they had forgotten the cruciality of class, but because they were influenced by the theological conviction that Christianity, as a religion of love, must reject a politics of conflict, including not only a concept like class warfare, but also the practice of aggressive trade unionism. Norman himself sometimes recognizes the hollowness of this rhetoric of reconciliation, as when he expresses amazement that anyone in the 1890s, a decade of particularly sharp class antagonism, could have spoken, as Westcott did, in suitably Pauline words, of Englishmen as universally acknowledging that they belonged to one body, 'in which the least member has his proper function' (ibid., p. 184). But Norman does not make the appropriate comment, which is that when Westcott talked like that he was not simply reflecting class bias, but struggling, not very intelligently, to apply to social conflict (of which he was aware) a theology of social harmony which had failed every class and political thinker who had relied on it in the nineteenth century.

Social conflicts which arise from straightforward clashes of sectional interest cannot always be talked out of existence by using the rhetoric of reconciliation. When Norman came to deal with the twentieth-century theology of liberation he was quick to mock the Colombian Roman Catholic priest, Camillo Torres, who chose guerilla violence instead of reconciliation and was shot in an ambush in 1966: 'It is sometimes thought', Norman wrote, 'that one of the reasons why young Latin-Americans do not offer themselves for ordination is that the image of the priesthood lacks masculinity—that religion is something for women. If that is so, at least Camillo Torres has put machismo back into Christianity' (see 'Political Religion's Imperialism', the third of the Reith Lectures).

The passage quoted brings out starkly Dr Norman's lack of historical imagination. He seems to have little idea that the misery of the South American poor is a fact of centuries' duration, not just of yesterday. As far as he is concerned, South America is a pawn in an international game of ideological chess, and so it appears quite reasonable to him to say that 'it is the foreign clergy who are everywhere noted for the radical politics', and that 'apart from the foreign clergy themselves, the others most noticeable for their political radicalism are Latin Americans who have trained abroad for the priesthood . . . [where] they picked up versions of Marxism from the student radical circles in which they mixed' (ibid). It is vital to Dr Norman's criticism of the modern churches that the effort of a small section of the Latin American priesthood to break away from their traditional identification with the ruling class—an attempt at self-consciousness on which one might have expected Dr Norman to compliment them—should be seen as inspired, not by distinctively Christian or religious sources, or by a particularly Christian understanding of the nature of man and of his social state, but by ideas current in the secular and all too Marxist West, alien to Latin America, and introduced there by corrupted members of the European religious culture. It is of the essence of Norman's position that men are free to become Christians in any social system, so that no revolution, Marxist or otherwise, is needed to make Christian faith possible.

The Latin American reply to critics like Dr Norman is that Christianity is not necessarily credible in any social system, and that it is as incredible in many parts of South America today as it seemed to Dietrich Bonhoeffer in Nazi Germany. The challenge to Christianity, Gustavo Guttierez wrote, did not come primarily from the non-believer, 'but from the man who is not a man, who is not recognized as such by the existing social order. He is in the ranks of the poor, the exploited; he is the man who is systematically and legally despoiled of his being as a man; who scarcely knows that he is a man. His challenge is not aimed first at our religious world. Therefore it is an appeal for the revolutionary transformation of the very bases of a dehumanizing society. The question therefore is not how to speak of God in an adult world, but how to proclaim him as a father in a world that is not human. What is implied in telling this man who is not a man that he is a son of God?' (see H. Assmann, *Practical Theology of Liberation,* 1975, p. 16). Commenting on this passage in his excellent introduction to South American theology, *Hope in Captivity,* (1977), Derek Winter said that in a sense the whole of Latin American theology of liberation evolves out of the attempts to explore that one question.

To Dr Norman, one suspects, this recognition of the incredibility of Christianity in an acquisitive, oppressive, even dehumanized society is no more than evidence of a faith weakened by Marxist analysis and by an indiscriminating, because humanist, compassion. 'Tolerance, flexibility and compassion are not distinctively Christian virtues', he told the Bishop of Worcester (who thought that they were) in the first Reith Lecture ('The Political Christ'). Nor are the values of liberal humanism: 'there are no distinctly Christian reasons for regarding its principles as more compatible with the teaching of Christ than other political outlooks' (ibid.). And so when Christians today seek 'a corporate reaction to what are increasingly regarded as collective sins—racism, economic or cultural exploitation, class distinction, the denial of human rights, and so forth'—something has gone subtly wrong as far as Dr Norman is concerned. He calls it the politicization of Christianity, the substitution of fashionable secular values for traditional spiritual values, and he treats it as though it were as recent and frightful a scourge as Dutch elm disease in the English countryside.

In fact, the diagnosis is familiar, but its implications are more ambiguous than Dr Norman allows. Here, a German example may make the discussion clearer, that of the Lutheran Pastor Kötzschke, who was dismissed by the Consistory of Magdeburg in 1897 for having denounced the evil influence of Baron von Stumm, a capitalist from the Saar, on the German Emperor. The Consistory said:

> The accused ignores the fact that the Gospel of Christ has no social programme. The Saviour did not come to increase our earthly happiness or to change the lot of unhappy working-men. The Kingdom of Jesus Christ is not a community made up of people who are possessed of a certain kind of social well-being; but according to Christ's own words, his Kingdom is not of this world. In consequence, the minister of religion must not set himself up as the representative of one particular social group. It is his role, on the contrary, to further the reconciliation of different, and conflicting, social groups. (Quoted in Rita Thalmann, *Protestantisme et Nationalisme en Allemagne, de 1900 à 1945,* (1976), pp. 79–80.)

And to Kötzschke's case, one may add that of Friedrich Andersen (1860–1940), who was Lutheran pastor at Flensburg (Schleswig-Holstein) from 1900 to his retirement in 1930. In his sermons he regularly denounced the 'Jewish influence which denatures the doctrine of Christ' and attacked the Old Testament. From about 1907 members of his congregation complained steadily to his ecclesiastical superiors about him, but with no practical result. In 1928 he was one of the earliest Nazi speakers in that part of Germany; he became a prominent member of the 'German Christians', the Lutheran movement which accepted the Nazi ideology. Nevertheless, the Schleswig-Holstein Church went on paying him his pension until his death in 1940.

In Andersen's case the Schleswig-Holstein Lutheran Church, anxious to avoid involvement in the politics of the 1930s tolerated Christian anti-semitism to the bitter Nazi end; in the case of Kötzschke the Magdeburg Consistory, equally anxious in the 1890s to avoid entering the political field, expelled a Christian-socialist pastor, thus contributing in the long run to the weakening of the Church's resistance to Nazism. There is nothing very new, in fact, in saying that the Church should keep clear of political action; there is nothing very new in saying that there are no distinctly Christian reasons for regarding the principles of liberal humanism—its opposition to racism, for example—as more compatible with the teaching of Christ than other political outlooks. Religious purity, however, like racial purity, can become a dangerous goal. When the search for religious purity actually serves the pursuit of racial purity, if only by attacking the liberal humanism which might work to ease the racial problem, it is the religious values which really come into question. Of course, one could still have become a Christian in Nazi Germany, for what the freedom was worth—though it would hardly be so accurate to say that one could have become a Jew. What kind of political assent, however, would or could the act of becoming a Lutheran have justified, once a man looked deeper than the shallow Lutheran teaching that a man was bound to accept and obey the laws and conventions of the society into which he was born? No doubt both Nazism and orthodox Lutheranism in the 1930s would have justified the kind of criticism of liberal humanism which Dr Norman is now, in changed historical circumstances, defending and recommending; but this still leaves one wondering what it is in Christianity itself which justifies this hostility to liberal humanism?

After the first Reith Lecture had been broadcast, James Hemming, in a letter to *The Listener* (9 November 1978), rejected Dr Norman's reference to 'the calculated hedonism of humanist ethics' as a most misleading statement. Humanists, he said, did not regard pleasure in itself as the chief good, but the fulfilment of an individual's positive potentialities. Moreover, humanists did not regard such fulfilment as selfish and egocentric attainment, but as the outcome of involvement with others in trying to raise the quality of life for all human beings. Humanists differed from Christians, he said, not in exceptional hedonistic tendencies, but in regarding global betterment, and the future, as essentially *human* responsiblities. Dr Norman said that the crisis of values which he believed had occurred in the 1960s ought to have elicited a clear polarization between religious and secular attitudes to the doctrine of man. No doubt, as Mr Hemming himself said, there were differences between the secular and religious points of view, but to *polarize,* and to say that one *ought* to polarize, liberal Humanist and Christian in the present state of the world's selfunderstanding does seem to require a specifically Christian ground which Dr Norman failed to identify. As far as he can see, 'the Church is in danger', and that is all that we need to know, and are going to be told.

If we put aside for a moment, however, Dr Norman's

obsession with the really quite unimportant World Council
of Churches, and look again at the Church of England, this
rhetorical appeal for conflict has its farcical side. One would
hardly suppose, to read *Christianity and the World Order,*
that the present archbishops of Canterbury and York, for
example, are irreproachably dull, impeccably orthodox (in
the Anglican Evangelical style), and rarely political at all,
except when Archbishop Coggan is moved to make mildly
critical remarks in the House of Lords about the behaviour
of some people on strike. Or that the Anglican General
Synod steadily refuses to sanction the ordination of women
priests, or any scheme which would actually unite the
Methodist Church to the Church of England. Or that as
recently as 1970, *Church and State,* the latest of a long line
of official Anglican reports on the subject, agreed that the
state was a divine institution, and proved the sincerity of its
affirmation by saying that the establishment of the Church
of England should continue as long as the state itself did not
choose to break the tie. The recent agreements between
semi-official groups of theologians from Rome and Canterbury on such subjects as the eucharist were so traditional
that the document on the eucharist was hailed by tra-
ditionalists as a great step forward, while 'radical'
theologians were left to wonder how long a united Church
would permit them to communicate. There is little sign of
the 'new left' theology which Dr Norman's anxieties would
lead us to expect There is no serious theological or practical justification in Anglican history since 1945 for the claim
that the faith is in danger. *Christianity and the World Order*
is ecclesiastical election propaganda, but the date of the
election seems to be 1968.

Certainly, the leaders of the Anglican Church do not see
their situation in Normannian terms at all. They are not
worried about the possible triumph of international Marxism. They are not much disturbed by the tiny theological
minority which produced *The Myth of God Incarnate*

(1977), or by the handful of English admirers of the liberation theology. As they understand it, Dr Norman has misread the signs of the times. What is worrying the Anglican leadership, for example, is the indifference of both the Conservative Party and the education experts in the Civil Service to the recent drastic reduction in the Anglican share in teacher-training, and the related disappearance of a number of Anglican colleges of education. Similarly, although the number of young men wanting to become priests varies from one year to another, the overall trend since 1945 is downward, and a number of famous Anglican theological colleges have closed since 1965. Just as alarming to the Anglican bishops has been the steady movement of the English Roman Catholic Church into the centre of the religious map of England; this reflected the emergence of Catholicism as the dominant influence in the religious sub-culture of the country, and as the natural religious alternative to Anglicanism (a change which marked the nullification of 'Protestant Dissent' as the other face of England's social personality). Dr Norman may see Anglicanism as threatened by politicization from the Left and theological corruption from the 'radical' centre, but what alarms the bishops far more is the drift of the Church of England into a pietistic backwater, where it will have little political, and, what is more important to it, little social influence compared to Roman Catholicism. From their point of view, Norman's Reith Lectures are more evidence of the drift which they fear. He is not making useful criticism of Anglicanism, either internally—where both establishment and the long-dead parochial system need to be examined ruthlessly; or externally—where what is needed is an equally ruthless critique of the relations between the Church of England and the Church of Rome. Instead, he is performing a ritual exorcism, with Marxism and mythology as the evil spirits; but these are spirits which have either to be refuted or ignored, they cannot be exorcised.

Dr Norman, in fact, has got his contemporary history all wrong. He has accepted the propaganda of 'ecumenism' at its face value. There is no important ecumenical movement in England—which is not to say that there are not gestures of middle-class religious co-operation, Posy Simmonds *Guardian* style, across the denominations. What looks like ecumenism at the institutional level, however, is no more than the evidence, at what might be called the 'diplomatic' level, of a power-struggle between the stronger and weaker elements in the English religious sub-culture. Under the strain of this conflict, which is not going altogether in its favour, the dominant group in the Anglican Church is not, as one would expect to find from Dr Norman's analysis, a league of 'radical theologians' and 'soft-Marxist' social-worker priests, but a hard core of stout old-fashioned Evangelicals and rejuvenated Anglo-Catholics. The reassertion of 'Anglican' identity, in its usual historically divided form, explains the pathetic inability of the Methodist Church to make itself acceptable to a working majority in the General Synod. Norman's writing, in which Methodism, for that matter, hardly figures as a significant living factor, religious *or* political, may be interpreted as an erratic by-product of this anachronizing revival. Norman, that is, has become the spokesman of a vague feeling that the time has arrived for orthodoxy to reassert itself, but his explanation of the decline of orthodoxy is wide of the mark.

At the theoretical level, however, there is another way of putting the distinction that Dr Norman is trying to draw. The distinction is not, as he suggests, between two versions of Christianity, the first orthodox, and the second corrupted by secular thinking. The distinction might rather be drawn between those who think that Marxism, as a system of ideas rather than as a system of government, is at least potentially creative (without therefore having to be regarded as either absolutely true or eternal), and those for whom Marxism (above all at the institutional level) seems to function as a kind of sophisticated alternative to anti-semitism. (Which is not to say that anti-Marxism and anti-semitism cannot be combined, for they often have been.) Anti-Marxism, that is, releases the same obsessions, fantasies and pent up energies of hatred which have so often emptied themselves upon the Jews in the course of European history. Marxism, like Judaism, is evil and explains all evil; like the Jews, the Marxists must be destroyed. Dr Norman is not what I would call an anti-Marxist, but when he says that the events of the 1960s should have polarized secular humanism and proper Christianity he seems to me to be revealing one of his primary intellectual impulses; he not only interprets history as conflict but (like Marx) he believes that history must be conflict. He has an absolutist's grip on Christianity, and he will allow no other claimants to the absolute near him. Marxism emerges time after time in these lectures as the one serious rival for the absolute: like Karl Barth before him, Norman constantly underestimates the attractiveness of the terrorism of the political Right. He sounds almost indifferent to the 'pretty normal coup' which overthrew Allende's Marxist government in Chile, because he does not regard General Pinochet's military junta as politically significant—only Marxism seduces (see the second of the Reith Lectures, 'Ministers of Change'). Of course, he may be right, but those who have followed his line in this century have sometimes been proved bloodily wrong, as Karl Barth was in Germany in the 1920s, when he thought that the soul of the German Protestant Churches was more in danger from the Left than from the Right.

The moral and spiritual relationship between Marxism and Christianity is more complicated than Dr Norman suggests. Until comparatively recent times western culture was based on the assumption that human life must be unhappy, was to be endured rather than enjoyed. In the Christian form of westernism it was held that if there was any permanent consolation or pleasure to be found, it would be found in religion: religion was the sure cure of alienation, as well as the anodyne which Marx supposed it to be. Dr Norman himself described this tradition with approval in his final lecture, 'The Indwelling Christ'; his understanding of it explains why he seems to approve of the Russian Orthodox Church, 'which is satisfied with the mere performance of worship': the Russian liturgy, he says, is not just a corporate expression of belief, it unfolds the very essence of the unchanging mysteries of transcendence, it is the disclosure of the very nature of Christianity itself. Dr Norman is asserting that alienation is a 'spiritual', even, in a sense, a 'supernatural' condition, which can be alleviated, if it can be alleviated, only by supernatural forces admitted into the human realm by the self-negating, penitent individual. One may act politically, as Dr Norman himself does when he contributes the 'religious' essay to a Tory symposium on present-day politics ('Christianity and Politics', in *Conservative Essays*, ed. M. Cowling, 1978), but one does not expect to change the fundamental misery of human existence. 'I do see humanity as rubbish', he said in *The Listener* (26 October 1978): granting a certain failure in tone here, he was nevertheless trying to speak in an orthodox, pietist, pessimistic tradition which slipped over at times into disloyalty to creation. Alienation could be ended only eschatologically; indeed, one of Dr Norman's more serious objections to Marxism as practical politics is that it actually increases the sum of human misery.

Marxism, however, symbolizes a deep change in the established cultural attitude of the West (and now the rest of the world—there is not really a 'Third World') to suffering. Popular Christianity never rebelled against suffering, but tries to work it into theological systems which would give it dignity, value, meaning. Marxism, on the other hand, as early as Marx himself, refused to accept alienation as an unalterable part of the human condition. For Marx, alienation was not 'supernatural', but a by-product of particular societies at particular moments in historical time. Suffering should not be accepted, or glorified theologically; as far as possible, suffering should be eliminated by tearing out its social roots. Marx rejected the partly Christian view that virtue (or holiness, in the more Christian version) had to be attained by self-mastery, because nothing outside oneself could be properly mastered. Instead, virtue (in the Marxist version, of course, holiness ceased to be a virtue at all) grew from joining the conscious struggle to free humanity from all that mastered it from the outside.

In this century, the quantitative increase in human misery has been appalling. Marxism has certainly done too little to reduce that load; at times, Dr Norman almost implies that the Christian Churches have tried to do too much. Of course, he does not think of himself as the apologist of suffering as such, but rather, as an Anglicanized Brutus who has powerful religious reasons for not killing Caesar and so upsetting the precarious balance of the present: 'we are up against the spirits of [fallen] men, and in the spirits of men there is no blood.' Perhaps he also suspects Cassius of being an episcopalian Marxist who will lead him into betraying the Gospel as well as Caesar. Religiously speaking, he is sure that he is right; and yet, humanly speaking, he may still be wrong. For after all, he is letting God off very lightly. Behind us in this century stretch the cruder miseries caused by wars, malnutrition, uncontrolled disease, and so on; then there are the more subtle miseries caused by racialism, lack of education, lack of opportunity—there are still nearly a million and a half unemployed people in democratic, peace-loving Britain as I write. Is Dr Norman's transcendence really entitled to contract out on the ground that 'Christianity recognizes that men are unwhole at the very centre of their being' (*The Listener*, 26 October 1978)? Is the Church, for that matter, entitled to contract out on the ground that God, humanly speaking has failed it? If one sees humanity as rubbish, this may be the only way to endure existence. I am quite prepared to believe Dr Norman when he said that he 'did not personally feel entitled to good things in this life, to the promise of truth, to an understanding of reality, or to a happy family life, or whatever' (ibid). But Marxism in its best days appealed to men and women all over the world because it said no to that kind of religious humility. We cannot afford, psychologically or socially, in this most destructive of all centuries, to let God off too lightly.

> You can hold yourself back from the suffering of the world, that is something that you are free to do and it accords with your nature, but perhaps this very holding back is the one suffering that you could avoid. Kafka, *Collected Aphorisms*

Charles Elliott

Structures, Sin
and Personal Holiness

THOUGH I run the danger of according to his lectures more importance than their intellectual content deserves, I have to start with a careful analysis of what Norman seems to be saying. (I say 'seems to' because inconsistency and vagueness in the use of key concepts like politicization' and 'essence' make it difficult to be sure that one has identified Norman's position precisely.) The argument, as I understand it, is this: The Christian faith gives us no direct political teaching. It is concerned exclusively with the pursuit of personal holiness. Part of this pursuit will demand acts of love towards others. In an increasingly bureaucraticized and politically-aware world, such acts have a political dimension. This dimension is, however, a matter of personal judgement in which the Christian faith as such can be of little help. Those with expertise in political matters, motivated by Christian love (detached, in some curious way, by Norman from faith) are those most qualified to decide the questions that arise. The Christian in the street may concern himself with them if he so wishes, but should not be cajoled by ecclestiastical authority into taking one view as opposed to another, since there is no Gospel or theological warrant for such direction. For Christianity has much to say about metaphysical reality; nothing about political reality. To deny that is to substitute materialist or pagan ideologies for spirituality and theological insight.

In his last lecture Norman calls for what he calls

'historical relativism'. That is not a term he explains and is therefore open to a number of interpretations. The context suggests that by it Norman means a recognition that present concerns about and approaches to, say, social justice or the eradication of poverty or the overthrow of racist regimes will, in the light of history, be seen as at best marginally significant; on average, wholly insignificant. Historical relativism therefore encourages a proper 'disregard of men's sense of the permanence of values'. Values come and go in the course of history; none is therefore to be accorded ultimate or transcendental significance. Hence (see above) ecclesiastical or theological authority should not invest such values with a transhistorical or parahistorical value they do not and cannot possess.

There are two major points that I wish to address. The first is the relationship between the Christian faith of the man in the pew and political judgement. The second is the transitoriness of values and Christian hopes for, beliefs in and experience of the eternal. Though I believe these issues to be closely related, I shall treat them in that order.

It is not without significance that, in an unfortunately characteristic way, Norman sneered at a phrase I used as a theme in my address to the Lambeth Conference, namely 'sin in the structures'. [1] I assume that this phrase aroused Norman's displeasure because he would wish to give the concept of sin a purely personal reference. A man can sin; a state or a bureaucracy or a committee cannot. To talk about sin in the structures is therefore to apply secular judgements to secular institutions and use religious language —language about relationships to God—of those (non-religious) judgements. 'These are' perhaps 'precisely the sorts of attempt at uniform political morality around which contemporary Christians are redefining the very essence of their religion.' I shall hold over a discussion of 'redefining

[1] Reprinted as 'Economics and Choice: The Crucial Battleground', in *Theology*, January 1979.

the essence' of religion for the moment. Let us examine Norman's objection to using a religious concept—sin—of a secular concept—social structure.

I have to admit that Norman was not alone in his objection to this phrase. In a perceptive and incisive personal letter a university professor wrote: 'The theological meaning of "sin" always implies rupture in the divine/human relationship which is personal, guilt-creating and capable of forgiveness after repentance. . . . In an important sense there *can* be no repentance for "sin in the structures". . . There is never any escape from the structural fact of Britain's contribution to impoverishment (of the Third World) and the arms game . . .'

I am not concerned to defend a particular phrase: I am much concerned to explore its implications, especially from the standpoint of the Christian in the pew who finds himself—as we all do, to a greater or lesser degree, whether we see it or not—involved in and confronted by social structures that have certain moral characteristics. In what sense, if any, is it legitimate to talk of those characteristics as 'sin'? I wish to make four points.

(1) Treading with the caution that befits a non-Hebraist and a non-theologian, I would tentatively suggest that *some* Old Testament concepts of sin, especially by the eighth century, had a community reference as well as a personal reference. This is reflected in a no less community-based content of such concepts as salvation, covenant and peace (shalom) which came to be defined almost primarily as a *community* state, rather than as an individual state. The NT understanding of this interplay between the individual relationship with God and the community's ontological status is certainly complex and not wholly consistent, confused particularly by different eschatological expectations. It is hard to conceive of the eucharist as having a purely personal reference, and as eschatological understanding

changes, so the notion of salvation regained some of its OT overtones. I would argue, therefore, that 'sin' is a concept that has a legitimate application beyond the individual. Nor is that application legitimate only to the fellowship of believers. To the extent that that fellowship, the Church, has a representative function for the whole of humanity (a subordinate but never insignificant idea in both OT and NT), it is not improper to refer to social groups or structures as being involved in or partaking of sin.

From this it follows that the Christian in society is not confronted with evil alone. The writer asks, in the same note, 'Why then should we not speak of "evil" in the structures? Evil in the NT is always potentially larger than the sphere of strict personal responsibility. One is not *guilty* of the fact of evil and one cannot repent of evil in toto. What one does is take up the weapons of righteousness and fight it.' Very good, but I fear inadequate, because it leaves evil disembodied, unincarnate, a kind of metaphysical, metapersonal imperfection in the way things are—'principalities and powers'—rather than as a result of an intricate web of choices, compromises and confusions, each of which stems from individual or aggregate acts of will. If one is satisfied with a Pauline cosmology, it will presumably not be disconcerting to conceive of evil as thus disembodied. Most people can (and, I would argue, should) no longer accept such a cosmology. We have to relate our ethical judgements to the cosmology we do in fact operate with in the rest of our lives. The 'web of choices, compromises and confusions' is part of that cosmology—and that points only to personal responsibility.

(2) That raises the second point. Institutions develop *personae* in a sense that is not poetic, rhetorical or metaphorical. The *persona* is embodied in precedents, ground-rules, assumptions, criteria, loyalties, common (and conflicting) interests and so on. These together determine the way in which an institution reacts to any

stimulus, challenge or change of circumstance. They determine its aggression, its self-assertiveness, its generosity, its time-horizon. They are not constant, but rather continually changing, adapting, responding to different forces, different perceptions, different interests, with the result that the personality of the institution is constantly evolving: indeed such evolution is a necessary condition of survival in the institutional world as in the biological world. Now it does not seem unreasonable (nor, I repeat, metaphorical) to ascribe to an institution—say a committee—which has developed personality in this sense, moral responsibility in the same way as to an individual. If that committee robs X by fraud, it is as morally culpable as if Y robbed X. If Mr Christian is a member of that committee, he is not only fighting evil, he is personally involved in sin. If that induces in him guilt-feelings—even though he may have attempted to stop the fraud—that is right and proper. He is in need both of personal repentance and, corporately, of institutional repentance. I simply do not understand what it means to be personally blameless (i.e. having repented and been forgiven) and be directly though corporately responsible for knowingly perpetrating an acknowledged misdeed. More of this below.

(3) The writer of the letter reflects Niebuhr when he says: 'There is never any escape from the structural fact of Britain's contribution to impoverishment and the arms game.' At least I take it that he is, perhaps unconsciously, following Niebuhr's tradition; since it does not seem to me that it is necessarily and *a priori* true that there is no escape. I do not find it inconceivable, for instance, that the U.K. should refuse to supply arms to overseas purchasers: unlikely maybe, but hardly inconceivable. So let us turn to Niebuhr, a writer whom perhaps revealingly Norman never mentions, despite his impact on Christian social thinking for four decades. According to Niebuhr 'the selfishness of human communities must be regarded as an inevitability':

he was convinced that 'there is not enough imagination in any social group to render it amenable to the influence of pure love' [3]. Thus social structures are caught in a state of permanent selfishness, without the possibility of moral growth—hence the title of Niebuhr's book from which these two quotations come, *Moral Man and Immoral Society*.

This kind of moral determinism has had a profound effect on Christian social ethics since the war. Owing something and being assumed to owe more to Marxist models of economic determinism, the idea that human communities must inevitably [sic] respond only to the interests of dominant groups has led to the view, partially shared by Niebuhr, that the only way (or the most direct way) that they can be made less immoral is by the manipulation or violent confrontation of those dominant interests. Leaving aside the philosophical problems posed by Niebuhr's position (and they are considerable), we need to face head-on the proposition that communities' actions and attitudes are 'inevitably' selfish—i.e. are determined only by the interests (whether economic or not) of those who control them. I find such a proposition so grotesque that it only needs careful statement to be seen to be false. Social structures vary greatly in their moral quality, their ability to take account of the effects of their actions on others, their use of non-mutual power, their readiness to exploit non-reciprocal relationships, their idealism. To say this is not to assert that any such structure is perfect, ideal or worthy of any kind of ultimate moral approval: it is only to point to the fact, which I take to be self-evident, that there is great variability in the way structures or collectivities do in fact deal with moral issues (which they may not in fact see as *moral* issues at all).

Let me illustrate this with respect to an issue that is

[3] Reinhold Niebuhr, *Moral Man and Immoral Society* (SCM edition, 1963), p. 272.

currently exercising the international economic community—and indeed some radical Christians of whom Norman
evidently disapproves. It has long been a matter of complaint by developing countries that the prices of their
exports both fluctuate excessively and have tended to
decline in relation to the goods they import. For example,
between 1954 and 1972 the terms of trade of the developing countries have declined by 0.56 per cent per annum,
while those of the developed countries have improved by
0.58 per cent per annum. In crude terms this amounts, over
a twenty-year period, to a huge transfer of welfare from the
poor to the rich—a transfer that far exceeds the real net
value of aid in the reverse direction. There is nothing that is
inevitable or inviolable about such a state of affairs: at its
heart lies a series of interconnected decisions by relatively
powerful people and groups about their relationship with
relatively less powerful people and groups. It is no surprise
to find, therefore, that the latter have demanded that the
international community at large, and supremely of course
the developed countries, so change the price-fixing
arrangements for their exports that the transfer of
resources from poor to rich is stopped. It became clear in
1975–7 that the developed countries were responding to
these demands in quite different ways, despite the
similarities in the economic and political interests involved.
To put it another way, an analysis of the interests of the
dominant political groups in Holland, Sweden, Denmark,
France, Germany, Canada, the U.K. and the U.S.A. would
not have enabled one to predict the reactions of these
governments to the demands of the developing countries.
In general the Scandinavian countries and Holland seem to
have been more successful in building *both* sensitivity *and*
reality into their political and economic structures than
have Germany and the U.K. I believe this is more readily
explicable in terms of the moral foundations of some
elements of the ruling Dutch coalition than in terms of

differences of economic structure between, say, Holland and Germany. At the other extreme the reactionary position of the U.S.A., Japan and the U.K. was indeed entirely predictable given the nature of the interests involved and their political weight. I conclude from this simple example that it is false to suppose that economic and/or political interests are so strong that they make it impossible for moral considerations to be heard, always and for ever. That there is a degree of determinacy (if that is not a contradiction in terms) is of course incontestable. But there is at the margin a degree of flexibility and adaptiveness which needs to be explained by reference, *inter alia*, to the value systems of the actors in the structures themselves. (Recall the discussion above about the components of corporate personality.)

From the actors' point of view, therefore, the position seems to me to be one in which there is room for a *limited* degree of movement, of flexibility, elasticity, adaptation. It is as false to pretend that he is caught in a wholly deterministic system as it is to pretend that he is caught in a system over which he has control. For both let him off the hook unrealistically easily. The first pretence is to invite the reaction: 'There's nothing I can do about it; it's the system which is at fault.' The second is to invite total moral collapse because, such is the nature of things, he can in fact not change 'the system' entirely and alone—and would be a fool to try in the expectation that he could. More positively, the fact that there is some marginal *but not unimportant* 'play' in 'the system' makes it mandatory to maximize the beneficial effects of that play. In doing so one will not turn the tanker through 180 degrees: but one may change its course enough to avert a collision. That is not a counsel of despair; nor, much less, a kind of rationalization of impotence. It has much to do with using sacramentally the grace that is given one—and also, paradoxically, is given to the structures themselves.

(4) Some institutions and structures are more open, afford easier points of entry and are more readily accessible than others. The same is true over time: structures may go through periods when they are more easily influenced and times when the determinisms seem to be much more firmly in control. For this reason, both Norman and Niebuhr are surely right to insist upon a degree of political nous in those who are involved in structural change. It was the difference in their ability to identify areas of manoeuvrability within the structures that they are concerned with that made Niebuhr so much more appreciative of Gandhi than of Tolstoy and his followers among the Russian peasantry. A flair for spotting what can be achieved; for judging the precise moment for political initiatives; for assembling the necessary components that will give those political initiatives a chance of success—these are the essential attributes of those who seek to maximize the flexibility of institutional change.

From this it follows that a degree of political 'feel' is a necessary condition for confronting the sin in the structures. Norman sees this, but draws the wrong conclusion: indeed he draws two wrong conclusions. The first is that since Christians do not usually possess political expertise, they should leave well alone. This strange view has been analysed by Peter Hinchliff in this volume. The second is that since Church leaders are not involved in political (by which he means national party political, a narrower sense than I have used so far) matters, they should not offer judgements on political matters. That is simply a *non-sequitur*. Bishops and ecumenical leaders recognize the need both to sustain those who are involved in institutional change and to probe continually the ethical frontiers of political action to keep in being a proper sense of the provisional and inadequate nature of any particular political stance, as Daniel Jenkins also has suggested.

I have been arguing that it is proper to regard the moral

characteristics of various social structures, and therefore our involvement in them, as sin—i.e. moral behaviour that ruptures relationships with God and our fellowmen. I now wish to return to the earlier question of the way in which the Christian involved in such structures, as we all are, relates his faith to his struggle within that structure. It is necessary to return once more to Niebuhr. Faced with the ethical problem of man-on-the-way-to-salvation and society stuck as it were in original sin, Niebuhr came to the conclusion, in a celebrated passage, that the 'involved' Christian had to adopt a dualistic solution. He had to do all that was in his power to sustain his own spiritual growth, but at the same time recognize that he was involved in and dealing with social structures that were incapable of such growth. 'Whenever religious idealism brings forth its purest fruits and places the strongest check upon selfish desire, it results in policies that from the political perspective are quite impossible. There is in other words no possibility of harmonizing the two strategies designed to bring the strongest inner and the most effective social restraint upon egoist impulse. It would, therefore, seem better to accept a frank dualism in morals than to attempt a harmony between the two methods which threatens the effectiveness of both. Such a dualism would have two aspects. It would make a distinction between the moral judgements applied to the self and to others; and it would distinguish between what we expect of individuals and of groups.' [4] Clearly, the necessity for this dualism stemmed from Niebuhr's view of the inevitability of the immorality of society. Once the contrast is drawn between the individual called to the way of sanctification on the one hand and society caught in the inevitability of its own moral bankruptcy, a dualism between personal and political ethics is rendered inevitable.

Conversely, Niebuhr's extremely pessimistic view of social structures seems to justify varieties of Norman's own

[4] Ibid, pp. 270–1.

moral relativism and the pietism that derives from it. For if all social structures are damned, one is not more damned than the other, and while one may take an aseptic interest in them—as e.g. employee, trade union official or voter—one can hold out little hope for their ability to advance the Kingdom. For that one looks only to personal sanctification. Paradoxically, then, Niebuhr's argument could be subverted and used to support exactly the approach that he was most anxious to contest—and which Norman has now resurrected, albeit in an imprecise and muddled way.

That poses the central question. I have argued so far that the variability of the ethical nature of collectivities, and the way in which those collectivities change implies for the actors choice and, therefore, struggle without any assurance of major or lasting success. That implies the identification of a 'proper Christian' ethical position in the light of which the actor undertakes his struggle. I have suggested that Niebuhr's dualistic account is not wholly adequate, because it is based upon an overtly deterministic view of structural change; and that Norman's account (to which I shall return) over-emphasizes the provisionality and interim nature of any ethical position, thus resulting in an almost cynical hyper-relativism. What I think we need to do is to reassert the biblical insistence of both Niebuhr and Norman on the Christians' vocation to sanctification, and *at the same time* ally that to a developing political moral consciousness which is both adequate to sustain actors in the process of institutional struggle and, simultaneously, sufficiently open to prevent the hardening of ideological arteries, which is the very antithesis of personal sanctification. In another context, I have referred to this dialectic between engagement in structural change and the search for personal holiness as 'radical contemplation'. It is radical because it calls the Christian back to the roots of his faith and because it allows nothing to be taken for granted. Thus

118   *Christian Faith and Political Hopes*

politically, morally and spiritually, it is open to the transforming Grace of God. It is contemplation because it
seeks vision that gives vision—that is the vision of transcendental unity with the Creator and the whole created
universe through which and in the light of which the vision
of a world transformed is granted. Clearly, this vision is
pregnant with judgement on the actor himself. It reveals
him for what he is and also gives him the possibility of
glimpsing all that he might become. It is, therefore, a
means (but not necessarily the only means) of personal
spiritual growth but it becomes too a touchstone by which
the actor is able to judge, either immediately or through
the mediation of rational analysis, the ethics of his own
political involvement. If I may quote from what I have
written before: radical contemplation does not seek (or
does not seek only) 'a kind of Transfiguration experience,
a glorious moment when the whole plan of redemption is
vouchsafed. In my own limited experience, the vision that
comes from radical contemplation is much more earthy,
more concerned with the nuts and bolts of a particular
situation. It enables one to spot the creative possibilities
of that situation, to see where the Holy Spirit is seeking
movement, to glimpse how the divine plan of transformation impinges upon one detail of the world-as-it-is. But
because the world is as it is, there are occasions when no
creative possibilities are apparent, even in the most perceptive and open moments. This raises the second function of contemplation which is the sustenance of hope in a
hopeless situation. This is not cheap optimism or a general
reluctance to face the facts as they are. It is feeding on a
hope embedded in the Cross and Resurrection, a living
out of love to death. As such, it is literally and properly an
agony made tolerable only by contemplation on the
enduring love of God for his wretched creation.' [5]

[5] C. M. Elliott, *Inflation and the Compromised Church*, CJL, Belfast
1975, pp. 139–40.

It may be argued (as, in only a slightly different context, it has recently been)[6] that this is an appeal to a romantic mysticism, because it makes political judgements overly subjective and possibly irrational. I shall wish to return to that when considering relativism below.

If this is even roughly right, I believe a less inadequate account of the relationship between personal holiness and social action is to be found not in the 'praxis' advocated by more-or-less Christian Marxists which tends to have an inflexible ideology at its root, but in a dialectial process. In this process personal holiness is not pursued in isolation from institutional struggle nor is institutional struggle allowed to become a kind of optional extra that those so minded can engage in as a spare time occupation, so long as it does not conflict with their real vocation, the pursuit of personal sanctification. Rather the one feeds on the other and both feed on the utter openness to the Spirit which I have called radical contemplation. This openness is not identical to Norman's historical relativism. It is much nearer to what David Jenkins has been pleading for in the context of theological debate in general. '. . .How can anyone who has received and shared a glimpse of the glory of God dare to believe that he or she knows exactly what God is like and precisely what God either demands or permits? If God does offer us "Theophania", opportunities to respond to him and become clearer about him it seems that this must enlarge us, invite us to live into the Mystery out of which we hope to live and be saved, offer us a dependence which does not trap us but sets us free, confront us with a demand which does not restrict us but which pushes us into ever widening fields of practice, experiment and experience.'[7]

In other words, a proper relativism makes ethical judgements relative to what God chooses to reveal of himself and

[6] See R. Preston's letter in *Theology*, October 1978.
[7] Editorial in *Theology*, January 1979.

his continuing creation and redemption, not to what historians think they can detect in human history. Historical relativism may (and only 'may') be an appropriate stance for the academic historians of Cambridge: it is not an appropriate stance for Christians who live, suffer and exercise compassion in the world. They have to take their stance from what they perceive and come to 'know' of the love of God, and the more they know of that the more careful they will be to keep *any* political or ethical stance as interim, provisional, open to further infusions of that love.

We are thus faced with two final questions. Is it true that the Christian radicals at whom Norman sneers so freely have in fact so 'redefined' the 'essence' of their faith that it has become ideologically closed? How can one live with an 'open' ethic with total commitment? The first question is essentially an empirical one, though it is not wholly clear what *kind* of evidence can properly be used in verification. There may be an epistemological problem as well as an empirical one. Of one thing, however, I am reasonably confident. The *type* of evidence offered in the Reith Lectures does *not* constitute adequate proof or even evidence for the stronger version of Norman's hypothesis (stated, of course, as a fact) in the first lecture. Snatches of WCC reports, remarks by bishops and archbishops taken totally out of context, gross over-simplification of complex arguments—these may be the stock in trade of the publicist and the entertainer: they do not constitute a serious approach to a serious question. I do not wish to prejudge the issue. It may be the case that *some* Christians (of both Left and Right) have adopted deterministic or ideologically-closed positions that betray a spiritual immaturity. But how many; in what circumstances; in the face of what alternatives; at what spiritual cost?—these are questions that need more humility and more penetrating analysis than they received in the Reith Lectures.

That takes us to the second question. There can be little

doubt that the temptation to attach oneself to a defined position—defined very probably in secular terms—is the greater the stronger is the moral, political and physical pressure one is facing. To put it crudely, those of us who have the good fortune to live in a relatively tolerant society and in comfortable circumstances have certain built-in advantages in the matter of maintaining an ideological and even spiritual openness. My friends in Chile, Paraguay and South Africa do not have those advantages: for them, relativism (perhaps most of all historical relativism) is a luxury that they would like to be able to afford. At the moment they have to live with the fear, the anguish, the frustrated compassion, the anger, the sickening helplessness. *Of course*, they 'ought' (in some sense) to be able to grow spiritually through that situation and achieve—or be granted—David Jenkins' 'theophania'; but it is a peculiar form of spiritual insensitivity that condemns them for seeking, in the torment in which they so often find themselves, a coherent intellectual position which both explains the world-as-it-is and offers insights into the world-as-it-might-be; or for longing for a fellowship of suffering through which both the suffering of the world around them and their own persecution can be made less intolerable. Calcutta, Dacca, Pumwani and Soweto are, in their different ways, *both* in need of explanation *and* in need of sympathy, compassion and costly action. I am unclear what historical relativism has to offer in terms of either explanation or co-suffering. As seemingly advocated by Norman, I suspect the answer is none. And a Church that set such store by historical relativism as Norman desires would have none either—in which case it is hard, perhaps, to see in what possible sense it remains the body of Christ. Rather than condemn those called to costly witness for failing to keep a properly ambiguous relationship with the political ethics that they find most appropriate in their situation, a more fitting response is to sustain, nourish, and support them (without necessarily underwriting whatever ideology they happen to have espoused), in order that they (and we) may live the faith more obediently.

For the task of being continuously aware of the provisionality of any ethical position, knowing that it inevitably falls short of 'the practice of pure love' and simultaneously being ready to live and die for it because, provisional as it is, it is none the less what we currently know of the love of God, can only be performed by the very exceptional—or the very blessed. We are back with radical contemplation as a source not only of judgement and vision, but also of enablement, empowerment, nourishment and hope.

Haddon Willmer

Does Jesus Call us to Political Discipleship?

I

THE present decline of western Christianity, Dr Norman tells us, is

> due to the surrender of its unique claims to an understanding of the nature of man. . .Christianity was once about human fallibility, about the worthlessness of all earthly expectations. Now it is seemingly preoccupied with human capabilities.

Again,

> Religion is centred . . . on the facts of human nature, and a human nature properly understood—from a Christian point of view—as corrupted and partial, so that, even in our most noble attempts at altruism, we find ourselves constantly involved in moral ambiguity and flawed intention.

As diagnosis of Christianity's condition, this is dubious; as theological perspective for Christian believing and action, misleading. Human fallibility is not to be denied, but it is not what Christianity is, or ought to be, 'about'. To deduce from human ambiguities and corruption the 'worthlessness of all earthly expectations' is to deny grace and make man rather than God determinative in the world. The substance of Christianity is not a 'view of man' but believing in God and participation in his life by the Spirit. Consequently, the pivot of Christianity in the world is not the fall but redemption. The fallibility of man only becomes the article of a standing or falling Christianity if God has left man to stand or fall on his own, consigning him, in his historical existence to find no freedom from corruption, no joy of forgiveness, no overcoming of ambiguity within the continuing ambiguities of life. That would mean that the fall of man is to be read as the historical implementation of unrelieved, apparently final condemnation. Genesis 3, however, in a way typical of the Bible, shows God making life possible and hopeful for man within the world even immediately after the expulsion from Eden. The fallenness of man is a universally pervasive power but it has been limited and unsettled by God the redeemer.

Some forms of Christianity understand redemption to apply exclusively to selected people, to the baptized or believers in general, or maybe to saints or specially favoured individuals. Redemption separates them from the present evil world, assures them of salvation and thus makes them effectively distinctive in the life of the world. Within these limits, redemption is genuinely believed in these kinds of Christianity. It is expected to work trans-formingly, perhaps even totally for true believers, giving them what the world has no part in because of its unbelief. This view has some biblical roots but its outlook as a whole is scarcely true to the spirit and scope of the Gospel. Those who think in these terms may well agree with Norman's hopelessness about politics, though the reasoning is different. The activist pietist is hopeless about politics when it is in the hands of unbelievers. The sceptical dogmatist, like Dr Norman, does not expect Christians to make a better job of politics than anyone one else. The decisive fallenness is in the human condition, not in some persons as compared with others; and politics is merely one way to play out the human condition.

Can we then say nothing except that politics belongs to the fall, while redemption applies only to unpolitical believers or an unpolitical hereafter? It must be admitted that the doctrine of the fall makes popular political sense. Few things teach hard-bitten cynicism about humanity as effectively as observing or suffering or engaging in politics. It then appears to be theologically endorsed by a doctrine which explains why the world is in its present state and which encourages acquiescence in what cannot be altered. It is odd to argue like Norman that the fallibility of man is a Christian truth so distinctive that risking unpopularity to maintain it can be a test of faithfulness to the essence of the faith. Taking redemption as a serious possibility here and now is much more likely to be a distinctive (if not unique) view of the human condition. In so far as the 'transcendent' is disclosed in the strange and the hardly possible, the unthought or the unthinkable, believing in redemption is a truer pointer to the transcendence of God than insisting upon fallenness.

There is a significant difference of emphasis between the Bible and Norman when he links political pessimism ('the wise aspirant to eternity will recognize no hope of a better social order') with God's otherness: 'Christians are those who act under the permanent rule that the ways of God are not the ways of men.' The phrase contrasting the ways of men and God derives from Isaiah 55:8 in the middle of a promise of a redemption to take form in history. Because God is not man, we may hope even in this world for salvation. Nowhere perhaps are the super-human thoughts of God read with such practical political hopefulness as by Jeremiah, when he advised the exiles in Babylon to settle down for seventy years, to plant gardens and raise families and to seek the welfare of the city, 'for in its welfare you will find your welfare'. For God's thoughts are plans for welfare and not for evil, 'to give you a future and a hope' (Jeremiah 29:4–14). If a city of exile may be taken as a biblical symbol of our existing in fallenness, we may take this advice to ourselves: because God is not as we are we may hope and pray for the welfare of the city where we live.

That will bring us close to looking for 'a better social order'.

Chistians are not exempt from the fall. They live in exile in a world awaiting its full redemption. They are called to think God's thoughts with him; to have the mind of Christ. Trusting in God the redeemer they hope for his redemption to show itself and they look to meet its coming round any corner. They are disappointed again and again: how slow they are to believe and obey and how powerful the outrageous and the banal evils of the world. But in so far as it is given to them to go on believing in God, they never make a standing compromise with their disappointment. They never allow the fallenness of man to become a principle determining policy, a fixed truth by which they can save themselves the trouble of hoping for improvement in the world. They do not accept as 'knowledge' what this doctrine of the fall taken out of context might seem to tell them: that it is futile to try. If God is creator and redeemer of the world, the doctrine cannot be treated as scientific political prediction.

The redemption of the world through our Lord Jesus Christ has not abolished fallenness 'at a stroke'. It has, however, given us the freedom to believe in God, to look for the vindication of good and to live in active hope of the real eventual reconciliation of man with God. Man, so Hebrews 2:5 ff. puts it, was made a little lower than the angels, with everything put into subjection to him. 'As it is, we do not yet see everything in subjection to him. But we see Jesus . . . crowned with glory and honour.' Therefore we are freed from the fear of death which holds men in lifelong bondage, keeping them back from doing the will of God. To live freely in and for God's thoughts of welfare is of the essence of Christian believing. The Fourth Gospel offers the same perspective. The disciples asked Jesus: 'Rabbi, who sinned, this man or his parents, that he was born blind?' Putting the doctrine of sin to work by itself, all they could do was to accept the given state of things and to find someone to blame for it. Jesus refused the terms of the question: 'It was not that this man sinned or his parents, but that the works of God might be made manifest in him.' Believing in God and looking for redemption to happen go together (John 9:1 ff.).

II

This believing must be more than having faith for oneself, as though what is believed is real only for the one who believes. For, as Paul said, the ground of faith is the love of God evidenced in Christ's dying for us, 'while we were yet sinners'. Our confidence in redemption rests ultimately on God's love for his enemies (Romans 5:6–11). Faith in such love cannot be genuine if the believer remains locked up in self-concern, be it never so pious. The believer who knows himself to be loved by God only because there is, in God, love for enemies, must recognize that he is called to love others with the same open boundaries, and to love them most profoundly by believing that God's love and redemption is for them also. Faith in God which does not reach out to believe and hope for the world undermines its own foundation. It can stand upon the love of God only if it obeys the outgoing drive of that love (2 Corinthians 5:14 ff.).

It follows that believing in God involves learning experimental and effective concern for others. Christian faith is properly characterized by a generous and hopeful sense of the needs of people and it will exert itself to use and invent the means of supplying them. Four men tore open a roof to set their paralytic friend before Jesus and when he saw *their* faith, he forgave his sins and healed him (Mark 2:1–12). A centurion asked Jesus to heal not himself but his servant: Jesus said he had not seen such faith, even in Israel (Luke 7:1–10). These stories are not themselves political.

If our reading of them is responsive to the love of God they witness to, we will be looking for contemporary equivalent realizations, which may on occasion be political. In these stories, faith was often directed towards physical healing; it was not restricted to 'ethereal' or timeless goods. Health care, which may be a partial modern equivalent, has an unavoidable political side. Politics works by inventing, nurturing and using relationships between persons and groups to serve human purposes, which may be good as well as bad. In these stories, the gospel of Jesus Christ is manifest in the making of relationships which are life-giving. Politics is not always life-giving or life-enhancing. The way of God's redemption in Christ has critical meaning because it was a discrimination in favour of some kinds of relationships and ways of using them and against other possibilities. As Charles Elliott argues in this volume, politics is about choosing between possible human relationships. The Gospel arouses in us the prayer for politics in which men are more rather than less enabled to live in love with all their neighbours, near and far. It certainly does not teach us that the relationships of people are insignificant.

We may be tempted to refuse to relate these stories to politics by insisting upon the letter, which is not political. So to limit their relevance to our action, however, is to come perilously close in spirit to those who criticized Jesus for healing on the Sabbath (Mark 3:1–6). As Jesus pointed out, the Sabbath was not meant to stand in the way of doing physical as well as spiritual good to people (Matthew 12:11–12). The day which was the sign of God's rest when his good creative work was done was not to be turned into a pious instrument of indifference to the neighbour who was, perhaps materially, alienated from God's rest. Few are nowadays brought by legalistic sabbatarianism into such ungodly callousness. But other forms of the restrictive interpretation of the word of God may have the same result. Excluding a political reference may be one of them.

One of the least disputed facts of the life of Jesus is that he ate with tax-collectors and sinners. It was shocking enough to bring him to a political death, for if sinners were religious outcasts, those who extorted money for the Romans and themselves were like Quislings.[1] To associate with them provoked all good patriots. Jesus did not shun the provocation: to eat with such people was, for him, a sign revealing the character and purpose of his ministry. Jesus did not use the following he gathered as a political instrument to destroy and then replace the existing government. He was no Ayotollah Khomeini. On the other hand, his work had political characteristics; it involved gathering about him a distinctive community and interpreting it as a critical alternative to other possible ways of being God's people in the world. And to be God's people in some way or another was one type of political option in first-century Palestine. The criticism Jesus made of other political ways was not based on a religious appeal to a transcendent, other-worldly, historically impracticable ideal. It was a challenge implicit in his practice. By accepting the poor and despised as full and worthy members of his incipient informal community, he at least pressed home the question: Do human communities have to be as callous, exclusive and unforgiving as they often are, and as so-called 'realism' says they must be? And, can the people of God be like that without contradicting their identity?

Jesus had a reputation as a glutton and a drunkard (Matthew 11:18). The pejorative tone of the comment suggests it came from someone working with other-worldly criteria for true religion; clearly Jesus had braved such disapproval, for eating and drinking had great positive significance for him. That does not mean, however, that feasting in anticipation of the coming kingdom of heaven may be taken to warrant conflating the Gospel with the modern pursuit of an affluent consumer society. In view of

[1] N. Perrin, *Rediscovering the Teaching of Jesus* (1967), pp. 102 ff.

the dangers and shortcomings of such society, as we have
learnt them, such a view would discredit the attempt to hear
the Gospel in and for our politics. The conflation is possible
only on a superficial, even frivolous, reading of the Gospels. In the first place, Jesus did not validate material
expectations indiscriminately, as the ethos of affluent
societies tends to do. The rich who looked for yet wider
margins of profit or security did not meet with his approval.
They fear to lose luxuries while the poor lack basic necessities or never get leisure from the unremitting and precarious labour for them: the two cases cannot be treated alike.
The human value of material things is to be affirmed from
the point of view of the poor. Christian criticism of ma-
terialistic societies where the demand for possessions and
power escalates out of control is not to be made by setting
spirit over against matter, God over against his creation,
but by asking why such societies make so many poor and
treat them so badly when they have them.

In the second place, the Gospels make less of the poor's
consumption of good and necessary gifts and more of God's
giving in and through Jesus and its significance. On that
basis, they are interested in the possibility that even the
poor may enter a community where they do not merely
depend on what is given them but are able to join in the
giving. For 'it is more blessed to give than to receive' (Acts
20:35). Jesus did not monopolise that happiness but called
others to share it. He warned those who would not rejoice
at his including of the outcasts that they were thereby
missing their calling and their salvation. The elder brother
had no prodigality of his own to return from; he was
brought to the crisis of his salvation by being asked to join
in the celebration of his brother's return. Even for the
prodigal there was more to salvation than the private return
of the individual to the father: the feast is a social symbol.
The elder brother's calling was even more obviously social.
He who never gets lost never needs to be found; he who

never went away gets no welcome home. Instead it is for him to go on living in the unbroken intimacy with his father by—and only by—being glad at the restoration of someone else. Unless he does that, he can have no real share in the father's joy. To be a son of a father like this is not a personal privilege but a social calling; it is to have a share in the giving (Luke 15).

When Jesus saw the crowds in the desert, he had compassion on them as sheep without a shepherd (Mark 6:30–44). This social image may imply a criticism of the official rulers of Israel, whom Ezekiel had denounced as wicked shepherds, exploiting and scattering the flock (Ezekiel 34). In the biblical traditions of shepherding, spiritual and political cannot be sharply distinguished. It is the kind of distinction which compassion breaks down. The crowds listened to Jesus till they were weak with hunger. He would not send them away, which was the only practical course the disciples could, or would, think of. They may have resented the crowds who troubled their Master, intruding upon their privileged relation with him. Disciples, however, are not just poor men made recipients of God's 'inexpressible gift' (2 Corinthians 9:15); they are called to share in the giving. 'You give them something to eat', Jesus said. It is not given to disciples, then or now, to make a meal for thousands out of five loaves and two fishes, but it can be their service to organize the people, making them sit down in some order (by fifties and by hundreds) and to distribute the food. In these respects, theirs was typically political work. We have no reason to despise people, God's flock, by etherealizing the story to make the hunger symbolic or purely spiritual, or by seeing the disciples' work as a model for nothing but later sacramental ministries in the Church. Physical hunger in our world is a complex of problems of organization and distribution. The earth has arguably the natural capacity to produce enough food for all, if we could work together and share it. The lorry drivers' strike in Britain has reminded us that having something to eat may be a matter of transport and transport is a political matter. If hunger has done more than anything else to make contemporary Christians politically minded, it is an effect in keeping with the Gospel. To engage in politics for a fairer distribution of the necessities of life is not all there is to discipleship but it would seem to be a proper part of it.

Such care for the poor preserves the purity and truth of spiritual worship in Christianity. Paul, in the earliest account of the eucharist, chided the Corinthian Church for not really eating the Lord's Supper because their eating was not really communal. 'In eating, each óne goes ahead with his own meal, and one is hungry and another is drunk . . . Do you despise the Church of God and humiliate those who have nothing?' (1 Corinthians 11:17–34). Instead, they should eat together in a way that 'discerns the Lord's body', a strange phrase which probably includes in its meaning noticing and responding to the Lord's real presence in the poor. Admittedly, Paul thinks of the poor members of the Church; and even so, he does not propose action to do away with poverty. He aims to ensure that the fellowship is not divided by the reality of poverty and the poor are not hurt. Whether those ends can be secured without wanting to do all we can to attack poverty as such is, sooner or later, an unavoidable question. Paul's argument is not to be limited by restrictive exegesis, for that would run counter to the witness he bears to the love of God. The spirit of his argument must reduce any distinction between the church's poor and the world's poor to a temporary, provisional tactical difference. The church must see its own poor as the beginning not the end of its concern.

Dr Norman treats the command to love one's neighbour gingerly, as being neither of the essence of the Gospel nor very practical in politics. The command is an invitation to participate in the love of God for the world and thus to come to know the love with which we are loved. And love of neighbour has been a simple and sufficient way of bringing many people into politics. It inspires concern for the poor, which Dr Norman approves. But the poor are many and poverty has deep roots in 'world order', so helping the poor has to be political. Then, too, the neighbour is not loved fully, as a person made in God's image, if he is made socially dependent on charity. Love seeks the neighbour as a real free and responsible partner in community, who is able to join in the giving as well as the receiving. Hence in some circumstances, if we would really though imperfectly love our neighbour, we may support some cause like 'one man, one vote', for that may symbolize and to some extent enable and require a society where all share in reciprocal neighbourly love. It would be silly to say 'One man, one vote' is the essence of the Gospel, but it is not inconceivable that it could sometimes be the appropriate, obedient response to the essence of the Gospel, so that to work to make it work could be part of Christian service which comes from Christian believing.

III

I am aware that I court the charge of politicizing the faith. Am I not reading the New Testament under the influence of 'present values'? In Norman's description, 'the true Christ of history' gives no support to my view, since he was, apparently, 'a man who directed others to turn away from the preoccupations of human society'. I doubt whether this is as devastating for my position as it might seem. It is well to be cautious about claiming to have the 'true Christ of history' unambiguously on one side of the argument. Being aware of the much discussed 'problem of the historical Jesus', I would not claim that my argument rests on certain knowledge of what Jesus of Nazareth was and did historically, though I think there are good grounds for being less sceptical than some scholars. The accounts of Jesus given us by the New Testament are at least in some degree interpretations of memories of Jesus; the problem is often to tell where historical memory ends and interpretation begins. Unless we can do that, we cannot be sure that we are talking about the Christ *of history*. In this essay, I have been working from the New Testament's presentations of Jesus, leaving aside the questions of how far and in what senses they may be historical. Despite the tendentiousness of his phrasing, it seems that Dr Norman also argues mostly from the interpretations of Jesus given in the New Testament and later traditions. He does not enter into a serious quest for the historical Jesus. So for the present purpose, within the limits of an essay like this, it is perhaps allowable to argue in terms of the New Testament presentations of Jesus Christ. They have importance for Christian faith and action, even when the question of historical accuracy remains unanswered or leaves us with a mixture of certainty and doubt.

When compared with the New Testament, Dr Norman's picture of the 'true Christ of history' as otherwordly seems one-sided, even off-key. He uses an ancient way of modernizing the Gospel to adapt it to a cultural setting which is different from that of Jesus in Palestine. He paraphrases the preaching of Jesus: 'Time was short; eternity pressed near.' But Mark 1:15 put it differently: 'The time is fulfilled, and the Kingdom of God is at hand; repent and believe the Gospel.' Very early in its history, the story and faith of Jesus were taken into cultures where talk of the 'kingdom of God' sounded strange or was misleading. Christianity no longer looked with the directness of Jesus for the manifestation of God's salvation in the impending historical future. So 'kingdom' language had to be interpreted, even translated, and 'eternity' language seemed to suit the purpose in the hellenistic world. All translations, however, are inaccurate; by addition and subtraction of meaning, translation fails to be true to the original. Translating 'Kingdom' by 'eternity' has had far-reaching effects on the shaping of Christian vision and self-understanding. Recently, Liberation theologians' criticism of western Christianity has fastened on the theological and spiritual consequences of this translation. But western Christianity's history has been marked by recurrent crises which show amongst other things that it was never happy with the translation. It could be disturbed by the exigencies and joys of discipleship in practice and by the work of historical scholars. 'Kingdom' language has not been wholly lost and it resists translation into talk of eternity.

'Eternity' is 'not-history'. 'Timelessness' stands over against time, likely to negate it. But the Gospels see the coming of Jesus as 'fulfilling' time, validating its promise in time even in the process of transforming and transcending it. Unlike eternity, the Rule of God can take form in the world. It can be spoken of in parables: the kingdom is like a farmer sowing seed, or yeast at work in dough, or a steward tricking his employer. How could there be parables if the kingdom were like . . . nothing on earth? Every time we pray, 'Our Father . . .' we share with Jesus in the profoundest of all parabolic statements.[2] So to pray brings every aspect of our being and life now in this world within the scope of the rule of God: 'as in heaven, so on earth.' The kingdom is present in signs which anticipate the coming fullness of God's rule. 'If it is by the finger of God that I cast out demons, then the kingdom of God has come upon you' (Luke 11:20). When the imprisoned John the Baptist doubted whether Jesus was after all the one he had hoped for, Jesus pointed him to the cures he did and the good news being proclaimed to the poor; 'and blessed is he who takes no offence at me' (Luke 7:23). Jesus asked for these signs in their fragmentariness to be interpreted positively, not with an outlook that negates expectations of a better life.

[2] J. Jeremias, *The Prayers of Jesus* (1967).

These signs should feed scepticism about talk of the ultimate worthlessness of all human values.

IV

The Gospels do not present a modern political activist as Christ; they do present Christ as one who calls us into a discipleship that may well turn out to be political. That need not give rise to the fear that faith will dissolve into politics or that insatiable expectations and confidence in human capabilities will displace God. Jesus confirmed the expectations of the people, going about doing good, but his way brought him to the cross. Those who follow him politically will not escape disappointment; they will not be light-headed optimists. The best way to prevent politics becoming the substance of faith is not to shun them but to engage in politics theologically with hope and love, for the more we hope and love in practice, the more crucial the faith will be, even when it has to cry: 'My God, My God, why hast Thou forsaken me?'

The death of Jesus may indeed be read as evidence of the essential evil of politics. The Cross, it might be thought, tells us the truth about the fallenness of politics, for there no place is given to God. Is a low view of politics part of Christian glorying in 'nothing but the Cross of Christ' (Galatians 6:14)? Furthermore, the Cross is not known in Christian faith apart from resurrection. Jesus, excluded from earth, was received into heaven; does resurrection therefore teach us to resign from the world? Such an approach may fit Norman's spiritual concept of redemption but it cannot explain the Gospels. It reduces the story of Jesus to two essential moments, cross and resurrection, while the Gospels have at least three, Galilee (as it might be termed), cross and resurrection. In the 'cross-resurrection' pattern, the only earthly item is negative; in the other, there is an initial affirmation of earthly life which is not deterred by its finiteness. It is no disqualification of the ministry in Galilee that it was short-lived, not eternal. The cross was implicit in the ministry, which Jesus did not seek at all costs to prolong. The cross was a limit intrinsic to the work of Jesus. Since cross, however, was answered by resurrection, cross may not be taken as a sign of the worthlessness and futility of the way that led to the cross. Resurrection is rather the endorsement of that way as God's.

As the way of Jesus in Galilee was always social, in the sense explained earlier, so the raising of Jesus from the dead is, in Christian believing, more than a moment in the biography of the individual Jesus. His is a life to be shared, given to all peoples as the promise and power of life. It is so, partly because it gives a sure hope of a future beyond history. But, in addition, it gives life partly because through it the way of Galilee is seen to be no dead end, but rather God's way to life, in life, for all. Resurrection is therefore in Christian faith a very earthy, history-making doctrine. When what might be termed a 'Galilee-segment' of our activity, individual or corporate, comes to defeat in yet another cross, the risen Jesus comes again, as the One he was in Galilee; in the power of his life he calls us again to rise up and follow him in his way. We are invited not to give up the world as a lost cause but once more to risk affirming it practically, in its historical and fallible impermanence, as it was affirmed by Jesus in Galilee.[3] So beneath all their differences Christian faith and political life may be seen to have a similar shape: a rolling cycle of limited but genuine affirmation of the human in the present, of defeats at the hands of the powers of darkness and of limitation by mortality, followed by new beginnings in which the affirmation with which the cycle began is restated in and for changed circumstances, not now in Galilee, but in Jerusalem, Samaria and the uttermost parts of the world (Acts 1:8). The politician often practises this spirituality better than

[3] W. Marxsen, *The Resurrection of Jesus of Nazareth* (1970), p. 125.

the spiritual people, because it is in the nature of the commitment to politics that apotheosis is no compensation for political defeat; one has to try again politically, as the spider told Robert the Bruce. Resurrection must be lived now in some way other than resignation from the world. 'He who believes in me will also do the works that I do; and greater works than these will he do, because I go to the Father' (John 14:12). These mysterious and alarming words refer to much more than politics, but to hold that in principle they can never be exemplified or realized in politics is in my view restrictive exegesis which may serve to quench the Spirit.

Often Dr Norman's most serious admirers and defenders are Christians with a deep reverence for our Lord or a strong commitment to thinking biblically. Whether or not they like his politics, they believe he is right about Christian faith. That for them—as for me—is the most important issue. I do not imagine that in a short essay (even if I had the competence) I could disprove Norman's view of Christianity and establish another. It is enough to have sown a few seeds of reasonable doubt and brought to remembrance, for those who genuinely care about these things, that what God reveals in Christ and what the Bible says may be more open to politics and more hopefully illuminating for them than Dr Norman has allowed.

David Jenkins

Doctrines Which Drive
One to Politics

Two things about Dr Norman's Reith Lectures combine to
provoke anxious thought and to indicate an urgent task.
They are their evident incredibility and their apparent
popularity. They are evidently incredible for a Christian on
three grounds. The first is that they appear to ignore,
contradict or distort the dynamics and symbolism of the
presentations of Jesus in the New Testament and of the
central Christian doctrines of the Trinity and the Incarnation. The second is that they appear to be alarmingly insensitive to the actual human and historical pressures, agonies
and longings which drive people to various forms of political activity, whatever may be the mistakes made by them in
analysis, expectation or action. The third is that they
appear to offer no help or guidance in working out a Christian discipleship, either individually or collectively, which
would be appropriate and responsive to our contemporary
world—or, perhaps better, worlds. Thus as a statement
about 'Christianity and the World Order' they are disap-
pointingly inaccurate and ineffectual. Yet they were, when
delivered, apparently popular and held by many to be
saying something that needed to be said. Moreover, within
them three or four notes are sounded, questions raised or
warnings uttered which are of central Christian and human
importance.

These include an insistence on the transcendence of
God, an attack on the all too easy moralisms of much
political and social thinking, the calling in question of the

expectations with which people tend to engage in social and political action and a reminder of the reality of sin. Yet in some discomfiting way Norman sets these valid reminders of truly essential points related to Christian doctrine and belief in a perspective that produces a travesty of both Christian faith and the contemporary political and social struggles which he is discussing. Therefore the important points he does make seem scarcely available for the urgent critical and practical work that needs to be done and this is deeply troubling. Norman's concern for Christian distinctiveness seems to miss what is distinctively Christian.

It is very troubling too that Norman's largely critical and complaining lectures should be welcomed by so many as striking a blow for true Christianity and as at last questioning a trend (towards 'politicization') which is held to be both merely trendy and deeply distorting to Christian faith. It is also troubling that those who have followed or set up this trend out of what they hold to be Christian insights and obedience should be, or should seem to be, so readily open to the criticisms Norman is able and anxious to make. In fact there are all the signs of a central disturbance and controversy about Christian faith and Christian traditions which need a great deal of clarification and evaluation. Norman appears to believe (and not a few people appear to share his belief and welcome his interventions) that he is re-asserting some central Christian insight, dogma or demand. If one is troubled by his lectures, their content and their reception, then this would seem to be an invitation, if not an imperative, to try to set out more clearly what Christian faith is and what are the opportunities and the distortions which currently and significantly affect our attempts to practise it. Why is Norman so approved of by many professing Christians when he strikes a blow for Christianity in so un-Chritian a way? Or conversely, what fundamental misunderstanding on our part is it that leads to some self-professed Christians, including myself, to find

Norman's overall sense and argument so un-Christian—especially when it is admitted that he raises some critical and Christian questions? We have some disturbing questions here which are not just troubling at the level of disagreements about Christian practice, although questions at that level are, of course, troubling enough. We are faced with troubling questions at the fundamental level of what is involved in and offered by Christian belief itself.

What is at issue is the doctrine of God. (Norman, quite rightly, raises questions about spirituality and transcendence, both of which direct us firmly to the ways which are offered to us of understanding God and of responding to God.) In the Christian Church, through Christian tradition and by virtue of our Christian faith, what are we invited to know about the God and Father of Our Lord Jesus Christ and what is pointed to or hinted at by the worship of the Holy Trinity—God, Father, Son and Holy Spirit? The most troubling thing of all about the general climate of Christian understanding in this country as reflected by Norman's lectures and much of the response to them is the weakness, among both 'radicals' and 'conservatives', of our explicit and articulated grasp of the distinctive understanding of God which is offered to us through our Christian faith.

We seem mostly to have failed to work out for ourselves our own effective version of that dynamic and all-embracing understanding of the living God which is reflected in the Bible and in the classical Christian doctrines and traditions. There God is known to be God. He is also known in and through Jesus. He is also known in and through the contemporary. The first and third propositions are typical of prophetic religion. The second is that which constitutes the emergence of Christianity as the fulfilment of this prophetic tradition. What is distinctive of the whole tradition is the unambiguous but mysterious combination of the transcendent otherness of God ('God is known to be God'—and not a feature of the world, the universe or of

human beings) and of God's self-chosen and self-willed freedom for concern with and involvement in 'down-to-
earthness'. Traditionally and classically Christians have believed themselves authorized to claim, and obliged to claim,
that God was free enough, mysterious enough and loving
enough actually to have committed Himself to His own
'personal down-to-earthness' in and as Jesus of Nazareth
who became Jesus Christ.

There always are and always have been problems for
Christians themselves about maintaining and understanding this unique tension, balance and unity between the
absolute Transcendence and the actual Immanence of God
but this is not the place to pursue them. (My own attempts
to make a practical contribution to these problems, and to
much else that is relevant to current controversies about
'God, Christ and politicization', are to be found in *The
Glory of Man* (1967) and *The Contradiction of Christianity*
(1976)—both SCM Press, London.) There is no need in this
context to pursue problems of doctrine and belief about the
person of Christ or God as Trinity because Norman is
concerned to recall believers to the distinctiveness of traditional Christian belief and I am concerned that his widely
welcomed critique of the contemporary politicization of
Christianity is neither consistent with nor appropriate to
the dynamics of this traditional Christian belief. The mis-
takenness or impossibility of this traditional Christian belief
is not therefore at issue in this particular argument,
although it will be a subsidiary part of my subsequent
argument that Norman's version of the traditional belief,
besides being unfaithful to the tradition, is also no help in
commending it as something which is or ought to be believ-
able today.

Let us then take for granted what I take to be common
ground between myself, Norman and all those who welcome his criticism of the politicization of Christianity in the
name of a reassertion of the traditional distinctiveness and

commitment to transcendence of the Christian faith. This is that the belief in the incarnation of the Son of God in and as Jesus and the symbolic doctrine of the Trinity, God as three persons in one substance, are truthful and point to revealed realities. The question then is 'What ought these beliefs to mean for us today?' What is involved in or implied for contemporary Christian faithfulness? My theological conclusion is that one of the things which these beliefs mean for us is that we are driven to politics or, at least, that we find ourselves in and concerned with politics. What this further implies about the 'politicization' of faith is indeed a crucial question which must be carefully considered after we have considered the case for the major premiss (i.e., that the traditional Christian doctrines of Incarnation and Trinity today 'drive one to politics').

A first point in the establishment of this premiss is pointed to by the inclusion of the word 'today' in the immediately preceding sentence in brackets. This is an echo of the third of the three propositions I have earlier advanced as being typical of the Biblical and classical Christian traditions of knowledge of God, viz: that God is 'also known in and through the contemporary'. I suspect that it is here that there lies the crucial difference between what I would claim is the necessary way of seeking an understanding of '*traditional* Christianity' and the way in which 'the tradition' is approached by Norman and, it must be admitted, by probably the majority of practising Christians in this country at least. Hence it is here that we begin to engage with the central question about who is misunderstanding the Christian tradition about God which I raised in my introductory remarks to this paper.

It seems to me clear that what the Christian Tradition requires *today* is not simply what has become 'traditional' within the various Christian churches and traditions, any more than what the Bible requires today is what has become regarded as 'biblical'. To require that God and our understanding of him should be confined to, defined by, or recalled to these traditions alone is to reduce God to the cosmic or super-cosmic object postulated by the adherents of the cult which lives off these traditions rather than out of faith in the living God.

An essential (although not sufficient) part of any knowledge of or belief in the God who is witnessed to by the biblical narratives and declarations is encounters with Him in and through our own 'todays'. This is of the essence of the prophetic tradition, which is not 'biblical' but contemporary in its formation and power. For example, the call-vision of Isaiah 6 is 'traditional' in the historical sense (it is formed by imagery with a past history and which had become 'traditional') and it is within the context of the cult. But it is given its demanding and shaping power by its relation to the contemporary, to the material of its own 'today'—the death of King Uzziah, and the political and social context of this, within which it had taken place. Thus Isaiah's vision becomes part of what is later to be regarded as 'traditional' and 'biblical' precisely because it reflects a development of the Tradition through a living encounter with God under the pressures of the contemporary.

Similarly, the classical Christian formulations of doctrine in the age of the Fathers (including those of Incarnation and Trinity) arose out of the Church both living from and giving shape to its Tradition under the pressures of and with the concepts of contemporary living and thinking. The distinctiveness of Christianity and its unique understanding of the relation and unity between God as Transcendent and God as Immanent, between 'the visible and the unseen worlds' (to use a phrase of Norman's in his sixth lecture) was maintained and developed by such risky devices as using an awkward and dubious term like 'homoousios' to stake the claim of faith to hold together the transcendence of God as God the Father and the immanence of God in Jesus.

And so it has gone on, not without controversy, mistakes and blind alleys, all through the history of the Church.

This pursuit of Christian faithfulness and exploration through 'the contemporary' at every stage is recognized by Norman. The published version of his sixth lecture in *The Listener* for 7 December 1978 opens with the words: 'When the political and social ideas used by Christians today are identified and analysed, it becomes clear that they are derived from the secular values of the time. This has, of course, always been the case. The main difference between the present experience of Christian adaptation and past ones, is that the culture of the modern world is becoming frankly secular.' He appears to interpret this to mean that every time Christians identify secular values or questions with theological values or questions they are thereby betraying the distinctiveness of Christianity or simply conforming to fashion. But is it truly biblical or traditional to give up giving full (but of course, critical) weight to the pressures and discoveries of contemporary culture just because it has gone 'frankly secular'? Isaiah could discern God through history in the time of King Uzziah. The Church can use Hellenistic foundations for classical formularies. But when we arrive at the 'frankly secular' God has either changed (i.e. not continued to use contemporary pressures as one of the means of his revelation) or been defeated (i.e. he can no longer bring about discernment of Himself through the contemporary once human culture has become secular and atheistic).

But the real question is 'Is it God or Dr Norman who has been frightened out of history and the contemporary?' If worshippers of God do not really believe that He is to be encountered in and through the actualities of daily living and contemporary history then He is indeed merely a cultic object sustained by a 'myth' which works effectively only as long as the myth dominates culture but which is simply a mere story maintained by 'believers' against the realities of the world once culture changes. The tangentially incarnate God of Norman's Lecture VI where 'the visible and the unseen worlds were briefly joined and the supervening force of the divine flowed down upon earth' is just such a cultic myth in this weak sense. It seems more than likely that it is because Norman does not like the times that he refers to Christ's teaching and 'its deliberate evocation of timelessness'. As Dr Willmer shows in his earlier essay in this book the gospels are much more about timeliness than timelessness, which is a notion much more definitive for the 'secular' and pagan culture surrounding the patristic church than of either the Bible or of our own times. The understanding of the Transcendence of God which has been distinctively typical of the biblical and Christian traditions has always been of Transcendence experienced in the midst of contemporary history and actual humanity. Without an element of this discernment of and response to God mediated through the pressures of the contemporary (even if, or, perhaps, especially if, contemporary culture and thought are 'frankly secular') 'traditional' Christianity fades from a response to the living God to a cultic practice privately maintained by initiates and little related to a gospel of salvation addressed to the whole world out of experience of a living God, both known to be Lord and whose Lordship is known to be expressed through the Lord Jesus. It would seem to be a failure to be faithful to the distinctive Christian understanding of God simply to complain about politicization and not to evaluate the positive as well as the negative pressures and indications which the politicization represents, both in contemporary human life in general and in contemporary Christian responses in particular.

Here, it seems to me, we come up against a possible failure to be sensitive to what is *humanly* going on in current politicization which, in the light of a Christian understanding of God in and through Jesus, represents a failure to take Christian doctrine seriously as well as, or as part of, a failure in human sensitivity.

In his second lecture Norman dismisses Marxist accounts of Third World conditions simply as 'the propaganda depiction of social misery and economic deprivation' and, in his fifth lecture, speaks slightingly of Soweto as 'an emotional symbol'. Now it is in my view true that propaganda use is made of descriptions of people's misery and that human sin is often manifested in the way expressions from political leaders or would-be leaders of concern for suffering and oppression seem to get lost in practice in personal seeking for power. It is also true that much vicarious and sometimes spurious emotion is expressed or provoked around various *causes célèbres* to do with Southern Africa or elsewhere. But a disciple of Jesus Christ is surely called upon to be passionately (and therefore in some way emotionally) concerned about the social misery and economic deprivation which actually exists, whatever propaganda uses may be made of particular aspects of it. Likewise it would not seem to be just propaganda or mere emotion for a follower of Jesus to feel some sense of outrage at what is reliably reported to have gone on at Soweto and at the attitudes and institutions which produce and perpetuate such goings on.

It may well be that Christians above all ought to avoid simple moralizing which locates all the guilt in one area and places all the expectations on one solution. Certainly no Christian or groups of Christians ought to indulge in self-righteousness, revolutionary or other, or to take pleasure in judging and blaming other people. But is there not a spiritual and doctrinal claim on Christians to be ready at least to begin to attempt to weep with them that weep and suffer with them that suffer? I did not use the phrase 'passionately concerned' just above as a mere phrase. To me it takes its reference from the Passion of Jesus Christ whom I believe to be, in some real and effective sense, the

Son of God in fully human form and person. The Passion therefore speaks to me of the divine commitment of love embodied in human flesh and blood. The infliction of the Passion may speak powerfully of the sin of men and of their fallen tendency to repudiate and even destroy the good. But the acceptance of the Passion speaks even more power- fully of the presence and activity of God who, in His love and as love, is committed to accept, absorb and overcome this sinfulness and vindicate and fulfil the human goodness which is in the divine image.

It is, of course, Transcendence who is loving and it is upon Transcendence that we wholly and totally depend. But 'the Word became flesh' and the Passion which is love became the passion of flesh and blood suffering to death. At least, such is the revelation given to us as Christians. The transfigured Christ became the disfigured Christ before he became the Risen Christ. If we believe that He is the cosmic Christ or that the very being and love of God is expressed in Him then a passion for people as they are in the hope of what they can be saved to become is both demanded of us and offered to us. This passion has a heavenly (transcen- dent) origin and a heavenly fulfilment but we can enter into it in a manner consistent with God's revelation of Himself through Jesus Christ only through the actualities of flesh and blood. These actualities include for us much social misery and economic deprivation, many Soweto-like places and happenings, the frustration of low-paid workers who then act to the deprivation of the sick, the old or the children under the censures of the more comfortably off and so on and so on. That is to say they include much that is inevitably and inescapably political. Compassion, which is an attempt to begin to be part of the passion of Christ and of the passion for people, cannot take us away from or above all this but only into it and through it.

The increasing politicization of our lives (or perhaps, the increasing awareness of an increasing number of people that much of life *is* politicized) is not simply a sign of secularized and degenerate times. It is a true 'sign of the times' which has to be critically, sympathetically and severely discerned to learn what is of God in it, what invites a deepening of our understanding of the human condition and what is part of the continuing effects of sin. To use the perspective on human affairs which is symbolized by the doctrine of Original Sin as an excuse for writing off all human attempts to better our earthly and social predicament or to reduce all political efforts to the same level of indifferent value is to trivialize the doctrine to the level of a pessimistic slogan which is alarmingly available for that type of conservatism or reaction which interprets realism as licensing acquiescence in the injustices and distortions of any particular *status quo* on the grounds that sin is inevitable and ubiquitous.

But this is a simple theological mistake. A properly Christian doctrine of sin must be placed firmly within a Christian understanding of Creation and of Redemption. We are to perceive what sin is in relation to the Glory of God, His commitment to the fulfilment of Creation and His saving work in Christ to redeem, restore and sum up all things. Realism concerning evil, distortion and failure is demanded but pessimism is exorcized. Pessimism arises out of the basic theological mistake of pushing God out of history and out of the mistake in discipleship which will not share in God's risk of getting close to men and women in their actual struggles, sufferings, and hopes.

While, therefore, we have to be realistic about human efforts and historical happenings our task of responsible theological activity is always to be asking what is it *of value* that is to be discerned in and through any historical trends or fashion and therefore what is to be affirmed. It is on the basis of recognized value that it is then necessary to go on to ask what are the risks in such an affirmation and the practices which follow from it.

Thus the contemporary politicization of life, with its accompanying demands for Christians to consider political awareness and political activity as a necessary, or possibly necessary part of their discipleship, individual and corporate, has at least the following positive features which can be theologically validated, whatever errors of uncritical acceptance some Christians may have made or may be making in current practice.

More and more people have invested more and more in politics because of a widely spreading awareness that all human beings are as human as all other human beings. Hence 'exploitive' political systems, or, indeed, all political systems are no longer taken for granted. It may be clear (in my view it *is* clear) that the mere existence of this awareness, with its consequent demands for justice, human rights, fair shares and so on, solves none of the problems of classical politics and economics. I also myself hold that hitherto available philosophies, whether Marxist, Liberal Democratic, Scientific Humanist or Conservative, do not offer sure guidance as to how we should now try to proceed, let alone safe guarantees of success. (In other words, I agree with Norman that far too much is currently expected of politics.) But the human significance of all the political unrest and aspiration seems undeniable. There is less acceptance of 'fate' and a much more widespread demand to share in the resources available to develop as persons. This would seem to be of the highest theological significance. If Christ died for all men, then the awareness of more and more men and women they they have a right or a promise to be human, i.e. themselves, seems a most significant development in contemporary awareness. It is not sufficient (for salvation and fulfilment) but, once it has occurred, it is surely necessary to be reckoned with and to be built on. To write concern for this off as trendy liberalism seems to show very considerable theological, human and historical superficiality. To feel obliged to write such concern off because of the inevitability of sin seems to show no faith in or insight into God's redemption.

Secondly, as Norman himself points out, much concern is now focused on the 'collective' aspects of modern life. It is not clear how he evaluates this concern but it would seem to be one which Christians need to take very seriously. There are fashions in sociological thinking just as there are fashions in scientific thinking but there would seem to be no sound grounds for attempting to go back on the general build-up of sociological understanding any more than there are for going back on the general build-up of scientific thinking.

In becoming aware of the existence and effects of collectives we have become aware of hitherto unacknowledged features of our universe and of our human living. We are developing new but necessary understandings of our society and how it works. We now know that any 'I' is both part of and product of a complex of interacting relationships and groups. These groups themselves operate as complexes of 'we's' and 'they's' which operate out of an interacting set of personal, tribal, class, institutional and structural factors. It is just unrealistic and therefore untheological (as well as unfair and impractical) to talk about the personal morality of a NUPE striker as if he or she were nothing but an isolated individual face to face with an isolated sick person. (This is not to say that there is no such thing as individual responsibility, but this cannot be followed up here. The point is about the realistic context and scope of this responsibility.)

Collectives are part and parcel of human living and especially of modern technological human living and things go wrong (or right) quite as much because of systems as of persons. This is a challenge to theology and faith and not something to be ruled out by theology and faith. It is also an inevitable pressure to politics because collective pressures, powers, influences and distortions have to be responded to by collective organization in order to promote or oppose them. Moral and personal ends and aims in and through highly structured complexes like a modern industry can be sought or kept alive only through responses which must include collective organization and political activity. So a great deal of politicization is a necessary human response and adaptation to the sort of world we now live in and what we now know about it.

As an extension of all this, politicization is also clearly necessary in order to face up to the realities of power. If, then, we are to be servants of the Kingdom, concerned with detecting or setting up signs of its reality in and in relation to today's contemporaneity in the same way as signs were available within the contemporaneity of New Testament times, we cannot keep out of collective and political action and concern. The prophetic tradition, the belief that Jesus is Lord and the classical conviction that God the Transcendent is God the Incarnate who operates as God the indwelling and interpenetrating Spirit all combine to drive us into politics (where we are anyway by virtue of our membership of our own society, whatever we may acknowledge of it or do about it).

Once, however, we are clear that a Christian theological perspective and a contemporary human social understanding requires this sort of recognition of the inevitability and necessity of politics then the critical questions that Norman raises become of quite central theological and practical importance. They suggest a programme for theological and faithful reflection, research and action which is an urgent necessity for Christians, and specially perhaps for western and for British Christians, as we find ourselves enthusiastically, confusedly or unwillingly and antagonistically, politicized more than we have usually wanted or recognized before.

We clearly have to face some very sharp questions to do with the Transcendence of God. Idolatry has always been a

besetting sin which leads again and again to dreadful destructions and inhumanities. Idols are not always just false
gods. They may be the promotion by absolutization of a
provisional and ambiguous good to the level of a god, and
this particularly in politics. The dictatorship of the proletariat can authorize any ruthlessness or self-seeking
power. 'From each according to his capacity and to each
according to his need' represents a goal which is both
glorious and necessarily provocative to repeated action
against persistent obstacles once they are perceived. To
redeem and renew the distortions and destructions arising
from false absolutizations of valuable insights we need a
clear worship of the Presence, Power and Promise who
relativizes every human activity and every created fact. We
also need the hope that comes from beyond us and makes
provisional every definition we make or every expectation
we entertain.

It is, likewise, also very necessary to re-understand and
re-affirm the Biblical and Christian insights about the per-
sistence and ambiguity of sin. Otherwise we are doomed to
a pessimistic cynicism, a brutal opportunism or a romantic
fantasy which hopes not against hope but against the repeated facts. Nobody is to be trusted, least of all oneself or
ones party, tribe or class. Power has never been used for
good purposes alone. The fight for freedom produces, at
least among other things, the opportunity for the fighters to
become the new exploiters. So the struggle is always on and
as well as politics humanity requires transcendence, grace
and judgement. But the question for Christian discipleship
is 'where are these to be repeatedly found?' not 'how can
we get out of it all?'

Such insights have further to be followed up to give the
lie to that moralism in so much political talk and implied by
so much political action and expectation, which is the target
of much of Norman's most pointed criticism. There is
no easy or direct·way of doing or being simply good in

the complexities of social, economic and political life. Righteousness does not lie wholly on one side, or, indeed, anywhere at all. Justice has to be sought but some form of production of the necessities of life has to be maintained whether it is immediately (let alone fully) 'just' or not. ('Man does not live by bread alone' but in this life bread or its equivalent is a basic necessity for living.) Freedom as such feeds no one and the provision of a structure for any society requires a variety of constraints.

How people who are convinced atheists can be sure that a proper ('scientific') understanding of the processes of history is bound to lead to worthwhile human results is a great mystery, or perhaps a simple and profoundly human muddle. How people who profess to take the Bible seriously can share in this illusion and further persuade themselves that there is anything in the Bible that guarantees human progress in the happenings of this life is likewise a puzzle. Achieving the moral or enabling the emergence of the truly worthwhile in the midst, and out of the midst of human affairs is a much more problematic thing than utopian or simplistic political thinking will usually allow or than political action on its own can cope with. Compassion which seeks to share in the divine compassion demands involvement in the human struggles which drive men and women to politics. It does not licence acquiesence in political self-righteousness and unreality.

This should be particularly clear with regard to the expectations often invested in political action. 'Here we have no abiding city' and the expectation that proper political activity pressed to its appropriate consummation will bring about heaven on earth or even cause a drastic removal of our ills is a mistake for which there is no sound historical evidence and no clear biblical support. Christians are called to an identification with and a sharing in current political struggles because of where we are now in our human condition. A certain politicization and a struggle to realize what it is to be persons go together. But the pressure to politics is this present condition, not a conviction about a guaranteed promise to follow from the involvement or an assurance about the theoretical future which is (dialectically or scientifically or in some other way) bound to come about.

Thus full and realistic attention has to be paid to the criticisms about over-investment in politics which Norman pertinently raises. But this realistic attention to the ambiguity, provisionality and risk of politics has to be lived with from the inside. Christians have to follow God in Christ in to the midst of whatever it is that now engages the struggles and hopes of human beings. Our dependence on the Transcendent is to be expressed by our dependence on receiving both grace and judgement in our involvement and through our encounters. Doctrinally and spiritually speaking it would seem that Norman will not allow God to get close enough to history and does not allow himself to get close enough to human beings as they struggle, hope and fail today. He seems to want to go back to an imagined past of detachment and remote transcendence. Christians can surely, in faith, only go on. This involves going through the 'politicization' which is now encompassing us, which holds much of necessary value, but which needs to be vigorously criticized and corrected, often along the lines which Norman sketches out. The Reith Lectures of 1978 could yet turn out to be of positive value if they are strictly taken as not normative but provocative.